WHAT PETER PASSELL'S UPDATED EDITION OF *HOW TO READ THE FINANCIAL PAGES* WILL DO FOR YOU:

- Explain every footnote in a stock quotation table.
- Explain the difference between "Bid" and "Asked" prices on Treasury bonds and notes.
- Point you to the best Web sites for tracking your investments and making investment decisions.
- Follow interest rates and the Consumer Price Index.
- Find out how much money a company is really making by looking at its daily quote in the newspaper.
- Know the different kinds of stocks traded on the NASDAQ exchange and how to tell them apart.

ALSO BY PETER PASSELL

Personalized Money Strategies

Where to Put Your Money

Where to Put Your Money 1985

Where to Put Your Money 1986

Where to Put Your Money 1987

Published by
WARNER BOOKS

HOW TO READ
THE
FINANCIAL
PAGES

Updated and Revised

PETER PASSELL

WARNER BOOKS

A Time Warner Company

WARNER BOOKS EDITION

Copyright © 1986, 1993, 1998 by Peter Passell
All rights reserved.

Cover design by Mike Stromberg

Visit our Web site at
http://warnerbooks.com

Warner Books, Inc.
1271 Avenue of the Americas
New York, NY 10020

� A Time Warner Company

Printed in the United States of America

First Printing: March, 1998

10 9 8 7 6 5 4 3 2 1

Contents

Introduction

Millions of Americans own mutual funds, stocks, bonds, commodity futures, options, and the myriad hybrid securities that are traded each day on the nation's (and world's) exchanges. Millions more, who stash their retirement savings in corporate pension plans, 401(k)s and Keogh plans or own life insurance, have an indirect stake in what is happening on the money markets. But pesos to popovers, not one in ten knows what the little *s* after the price of a listed stock means, why the Standard and Poor's 500 sometimes goes down when the Dow Jones Industrial Average goes up, or why Wall Street treats the announcement of the last month's change in the Producer

Price Index the way the ancient Greeks treated interpretations of sheep entrails by the Oracle of Delphi.

Anyone who really wants to know can always find out. An afternoon at the library, a night course at a community college, or an investment in $50 worth of stock market tomes will do the trick. But it's hard and not always rewarding work, often almost as much fun as preparing your taxes or having dinner with Harry, your know-it-all cousin who claims to have never missed a turn in the market.

Enter *How to Read the Financial Pages,* a very short, very affordable guide that delivers just what it claims.

Part One: THE TABLES translate the daily financial listings from the newspaper and add some tips on how to read between the lines. Mutual funds, the meat and potatoes for the average investor, come first. But stocks and bonds are included, of course. And the financial stuff—index options, commodity futures, foreign exchange, and the like—are there, too.

Part Two: THE NUMBERS explain what commonly cited statistics, ranging from the Consumer Price Index to daily volume on the New York Stock Exchange, really mean, and how they may affect your investments.

Part Three: THE WEB lists a dozen or so sites on the Internet that offer up-to-the-minute information on investing. Most are free; all are worth the trouble to check out.

Read the book straight through in a few hours, if you are a glutton for punishment. Or just keep it around as a reference. *How to Read the Financial Pages* doesn't provide the names of 21 mutual funds guaranteed to stay ahead of the market. Nor is it full of gossip about rich people that will make you the life of the party. But it certainly does offer easy-to-follow information on personal finances that you must have in order to stay ahead of the game.

Getting Started

You can't tell the players (or, in this case, the payers) without a scorecard. But which scorecard?

Thanks to increased interest on the part of readers, especially the baby boomers who are beginning to face the cool realities of retirement down the road, newspapers have improved their coverage of business and finance. The basic securities market tables, revised for easier use in the early 1990s, look pretty much the same no matter where you find them. That's because all newspapers print the same data, compiled by the same computers, and transmitted by the same wire services. And for many investors, the tables, charts, and general business reporting in their morning papers will provide all they need to keep up.

In fact the most ambitious papers, including the *Atlanta Journal and Constitution, Boston Globe, Los Angeles Times, Miami Herald, Milwaukee Journal,* and *San Jose Mercury,* offer something the national dailies can't:

local business news. If you hunger for more, though, try one of these:

The *Wall Street Journal.* The most complete and accurate coverage of business news to be found, the *Journal* doesn't have any real competitors. The paper's only drawback is its bulk. Sixty to seventy pages of business and economics can be a time-consuming and yes, a boring way to begin the day. Happily, though, the *Journal* now comes in three sections, with all the hard-core financial stuff in one handy package called "Money and Investing." Edited in New York but printed regionally, the *Wall Street Journal* can be ordered for morning delivery in much of the country. Separate European and Asian editions focus on continental news.

The *Financial Times.* Though unfamiliar to most Americans, the London-edited (but American printed) *Financial Times* is a window on business with a distinctively European outlook. This emphasis on Europe and highly opinionated columns make the *Financial Times* quite useful for investors in foreign securities. Note, too, that the distinctively colored (pink) paper provides a very different perspective on what's happening in America—a useful trait at a time when financial markets have truly become global.

The *New York Times.* The *Times* Business Day section on weekdays offers a compromise between the everything-you-did-or-didn't-want-to-know coverage of the *Wall Street Journal* and the once-over-lightly, courtesy-of-the-wire-services coverage of most local papers. The *Times* Sunday Business Section is really a personal finance magazine, with lots of stories and columns on taxes, mutual funds, and the like. Both have been given facelifts in recent years, making them far more readable than in the bad old days. Like the man said, "read 'em again for the first time."

USA Today. Built around the concept of "less is more," the national newspaper published by the Gannett chain covers a lot of business and economics in a small space. Once referred to in the media biz as McPaper, nobody's laughing at the easy reading, jargon-free style anymore. The downside: USA Today is very light on securities listings. Those who follow the complicated stuff will have to go elsewhere.

Investor's Daily. Unlike the Journal or the New York Times, Investor's Daily doesn't try to cover broad issues of public policy with any depth. The emphasis is on the very readable detailed tables and interpretation of events that market professionals need to do their jobs well. This paper is available in big cities and airports and wherever true stock market junkies congregate.

Barron's. An authoritative, immensely influential weekly in tabloid form, published by the nice folks at Dow Jones who bring you the Wall Street Journal. Once narrowly aimed at professionals—the tables in the back are a thing to behold—it has been spruced up without dumbing down in recent years. It's worth at least an occasional look if you want to see how the pros interpret the ups and downs of the markets.

PART ONE

The Tables

New York and American Stock Exchange Composite Transactions

With a handful of exceptions (Apple Computer being the most well-known) the stocks of most large, publicly owned corporations are traded on either the New York Stock Exchange or the American Stock Exchange. There is more status in being listed on the New York Exchange only because the minimum requirements for the total value of outstanding shares and the number of stockholders are somewhat tougher. But from the perspective of a stock buyer the only difference of consequence is the higher trading volume on the NYSE, which makes it a bit easier to buy or sell large quantities of stocks without affecting the price very much.

Both exchanges have fancy computer systems for executing orders and assuring that all customers are treated equally. Both do a sound job of policing brokers to keep them from stealing your money or finding legal means to the same end. And, both report transactions in similar ways, so if you understand the listings for one, you understand both.

The tables in the morning papers are based on all trading activity during the previous day. Afternoon papers—the few that survive—sometimes limit their reports to part of the day's trading. But all listings are composites: if a stock is traded on a regional exchange as well as one of the national exchanges, the figures for the NYSE and the ASE include all trading.

Column 1. The highest price paid for Bell South stock in the previous year was $45.50 while the lowest was $34.25. Most stocks are priced in eighths of a dollar. When stocks trade for very low prices, though, the variations can be in 16ths or even 32nds of a dollar.

Column 2. Corporate names are usually obvious from their abbreviations. But not always. Bet you can't guess what DEGpGlb or VnKmACFLOp stand for. Boldface type indicates very large increases or decreases in price that day, while a small arrow pointing up (or down) indicates a 52-week high (or low). Underlining means unusually heavy volume of trading, often the result of dramatic news about the company's prospects or speculation that the company is considering a merger.

Note the "pf" following the Citicorp entry. This means the shares are preferred stock, guaranteeing owners will receive a dividend before cash is paid out to other share-

(TABLE 1)

EXCHANGE STOCKS*

1		2	3	4	5	6	7	8		9	10
52 Weeks Hi	Lo	Stock	Sym	Div	Yld %	PE	Vol 100s	Hi	Lo	Close	Net Chg
45½	34¼	BellSouth	BLS	1.44	3.5	19	6540	42	41¼	42	+½
95	83⅞	Citicorp pf		6.00	6.4	—	17	93½	93¼	93½	—
10⅛	**3**	**MedialLogic**	**TST**	**—**	**—**	**dd**	**545**	**3⅛**	**2¾**	**3**	**-⅛**

*Transaction information for illustration only.

holders. A variety of other footnotes are sometimes found here, including:

cld—The stock is a preferred issue, and the company has exercised its right to redeem it for cash at a fixed price.

n—The stock was issued within the last 52 weeks and the high and low prices thus refer to a shorter period.

s—The stock has "split." Owners have been issued additional shares in proportion to their current holdings sometime in the previous year.

pp—A "partly paid" share, for which owners will have to make additional payments in order to claim full rights of ownership.

pr—Some ownership preference, such as a claim on dividends before the corporation can be merged or the company sells more stock, is attached to the shares.

un—Stands for "units," and implies that something else of value—say the right to buy two additional shares at a fixed price—is part of a package that includes the share of stock.

rt—Not a share, but the right to buy a share at a specified price, typically below the market price of the stock when the right was issued. Typically, rights expire in a brief period, say two to four weeks.

wt—Not a share, but the right to buy a share of stock at the preset price. In contrast to a "right," a warrant typically has a very long lifetime.

vj—Indicates the company is in bankruptcy. Shares of companies in bankruptcy freely trade until the company is liquidated, and may be valuable if the company is reorganized in a way that grants some claims to the owners of the stock.

g—Dividends and earnings are reported in Canadian dollars, almost certainly because the company is Canadian. Stock prices, by contrast, are always in U.S. dollars.

Column 3. The "stock ticker" symbol for the shares. Handy to know if you want to get the current price of a share from an automated telephone or Internet system.

Column 4. The dividend per share paid to stockholders at an annualized rate. Thus if a company paid 40 cents per share in the latest quarter, the dividend would be listed as 1.60. Lots of stocks don't pay any dividends at all, sometimes because they don't have any earnings, sometimes because they are reserving the income for additional capital investments. A variety of exceptions are indicated by footnotes:

a—An extra dividend was paid in the past year but is not included in the annualized figure.

b—A dividend in the form of stock was also paid but is not included in the figure.

c—A "liquidating" dividend returning corporate assets to the shareholders, say, when a company sells a division and distributes the proceeds, or when it goes bankrupt.

e—Sum of dividends paid in the past 12 months, rather than the annualized rate based on the last dividend.

f—The current annual dividend rate was increased by the last dividend announcement.

i—The sum of dividends paid after the stock split.

j—The dividends paid in the past year in which the most recent dividend was omitted or deferred.

m—The current annualized dividend rate that was decreased by the last dividend announcement.

p—The current dividend. The annual rate is not known because the company has not been paying dividends for a full year.

r—A cash dividend paid in the last 12 months and a stock dividend also paid.

t—Paid in stock; valued in terms of cash at the stock price when the dividend was distributed.

Column 5. The percentage yield indicating the ratio of the annualized dividend divided by the closing price of the stock. High yields don't necessarily make a stock a good buy because the market may be anticipating a dividend cut in the future. By the same token, low yields don't make a stock a bad buy because many companies with good earnings prospects either don't have the cash to pay dividends or prefer to reinvest the money in the business.

Column 6. The price-to-earnings ratio reveals the stock's current price divided by the earnings reported by the company over the past year. High PE ratios suggest that the market expects corporate earnings to grow rapidly, while a low PE suggests the company's earnings are expected to decline or remain stagnant. Other factors, though, also affect PEs. Rising interest rates, for example, tend to reduce PEs because investors have the alternative of earning higher returns on fixed-income securities such as bonds and bank deposits.

Some relevant footnotes:

q—The stock is a "closed end" mutual fund for which a PE ratio has no meaning and is thus not calculated.

cc—The PE ratio exceeds 99, which generally implies that current earnings are a small token of future earnings anticipated by investors.

dd—The company lost money in the last 12 months, making the PE ratio meaningless.

Column 7. The volume of shares traded, measured in hundreds. In the example on page 5, investors bought and sold 654,000 shares of Bell South stock. Note that heavy volumes of trading make a stock "liquid"—easy to buy or sell without affecting the price. Some footnotes:

x—This is the first day the stock was sold without the right to the latest dividend: The price change listed in column 10 reflects this new status.

y—The total number of shares traded, rather than trades in hundreds. The stock was sold without rights to the latest dividend.

z—Sales are in total shares, rather than in hundreds.

Column 8. The high and low prices on sales during the trading day. A large difference between the high and low usually means the stock price was affected by news during the day—reports of a takeover bid or a big order from a major client. Or it simply may mean that the stock is lightly traded, and sales could only be completed by sharply raising or lowering the price.

Column 9. The price at which the last transaction of the day was completed. Since your transaction was probably not the last, it is very likely that you paid or received different terms if you traded the stock on this day. Exchange rules require brokers to get you the best possible deal available at the time you trade.

Column 10. The change in price between the last trade today and the last trade yesterday.

American Stock Exchange Emerging Issues

At the tail end of the American Stock Exchange listings are a few dozen stocks separately listed as "Amex Emerging Issues." These are stocks that do not meet the Amex's regular minimum qualifications for listing—in particular, a pre-tax annual income of $750,000 and a minimum share price of $3 at the time of initial listing.

Why, then, has the Amex decided to make special room for these stocks?

Glad you asked. The Amex says it is trying to give a boost to medium-sized companies with good growth potential. Others think it has more to do with the Amex's quest for new business at a time when competition between the exchanges is especially fierce.

Whatever the reason, it makes sense to be a bit wary of these stocks—especially if a brokerage house salesman

11

whom you've never met calls with a hot tip on one of them. They are all lightly traded issues of companies with less than established earnings records, and are thus susceptible to price manipulation by unscrupulous brokers.

NASDAQ Over-the-Counter National Market Issues

Publicly owned companies that can't or don't want to meet the size and disclosure requirements of the New York, American, or regional exchanges are traded "over the counter." The over-the-counter market isn't a physical place like the other stock exchanges. It is a network of brokers who belong to the National Association of Securities Dealers and "make markets" the way specialists do on the floor of the organized stock exchanges—that is, they buy selected stocks when there are no other buyers.

A few decades ago the network operated very informally, depending on mimeographed sheets of buy and sell offers that were produced after trading hours and distributed to dealers the next morning. The actual trading was done by the telephone. Since the 1970s, though, over-the-counter dealers have been tied together by an automated quotation computer system, known as NASDAQ. Trading itself is not automated; that still depends on brokers talking to each other on the telephone. But each broker now has a computer terminal on his or her desk that shows the highest bid price and lowest asking price in the system for several thousand stocks.

Of the 30,000 stocks available over the counter, figures for roughly 1,500 of the most actively traded are reported daily as NASDAQ National Market Issues. In most papers, NASDAQ National Market Issues are now identical to the listings for the American and New York exchanges.

A supplementary list of a few hundred lightly traded NASDAQ stocks is often printed, too. But, here, the tables contain only the highest bid and lowest sale offer, and sometimes the volume of sales.

The *Wall Street Journal* has expanded its NASDAQ National Market Issue listings to include the four-letter shorthand for the stock's name, used in the NASDAQ computers. In some cases, there is a fifth letter attached to the symbol which defines special conditions or restrictions on the listed security.

For example, COGN stands for the Cognos Corporation. But the listing shows it as COGNF, with the F showing it is a foreign corporation. Here's a list of the most frequently used fifth letters:

A or B. The class of stock. Some companies issue two classes of common stock, whose owners have, say, different rights to elect corporate directors or restrictions on who may own the shares. Make sure you know what these differences are before you buy.

C. Temporarily exempted from NASDAQ listing qualifications. Unlike the New York and American stock exchanges, the NASDAQ is not fussy about minimum assets or profits when companies apply for listing. Don't even consider buying a company that has yet to meet the minimum unless you know why.

E. Delinquent in legal filings required by the government for public sale on any exchange. What goes for C, goes double for E.

F. A foreign corporation, one that operates under the rules of another government. Such companies are still obliged to meet minimum disclosure requirements set by the Securities and Exchange commission.

G. Convertible Bond. Like any bond, a convertible bond obliges the issuer to pay interest on terms set down in the agreement. Unlike ordinary bonds, however, convertibles may be exchanged for stock at a specified conversion rate—say, one bond for 27 shares. This gives the owner the best of both worlds: a guaranteed annual return (provided the company remains solvent) plus a chance to participate in the gain if the stock value rises. Of course, you pay for what you get: Convertibles provide lower rates of interest than ordinary bonds.

K. Non-Voting Stock. These shares do not carry the right to elect corporate directors. Companies issue them in order to raise capital without risking loss of control of the business to outsiders. Other things being equal, they aren't as valuable as voting shares.

P. Preferred Stock. A preferred stock is a cross between a stock and a bond. Unlike bond owners, owners are not legally entitled to a specified annual payment. And unlike common stock owners, they do not have the right to vote for corporate boards. But preferred stock owners must be paid specified dividends before the common stock owners are handed a single penny. And typically, this obligation is cumulative: If the company fails to pay the preferred dividend for six years running, they must pay a full six years' worth of preferred dividends before issuing a common stock dividend.

Q. In bankruptcy proceedings. Stocks trade even after the company goes bankrupt because buyers speculate that the company will be worth something after the creditors are paid off. This is dangerous territory for amateurs: look before you leap.

R. Rights. When companies decide to issue new shares they often give existing shareholders the right to buy the shares for a brief period—a month or so—at a specified price. If this price is below the market value, the rights have a value in themselves. Rights are generally freely tradable.

V. When issued. Securities are sometimes bought and sold before they are issued. A company might, for example, announce that it is issuing a stock dividend. Those who expect to receive the new shares can sell them immediately, eliminating the risk that the stock price will fall in the meantime.

W. Warrants. Like rights, warrants entitle the holders to purchase shares at a specified price. Warrants, however, are entitlements that last for years—or even indefinitely. They usually are thrown in as a sweetener when companies issue new bonds or preferred stock.

Y. American Depository Receipt. These are stocks in every sense but the legal sense. They are receipts proving the stock is in the custody of an American bank: the owner of the receipt is legally entitled to any dividends, or any other benefit granted to the stockholder by the company. Why the rigamirole? It is a way for foreign companies to trade their stock on U.S. exchanges without meeting the onerous disclosure requirements of the U.S. securities laws.

New York and American Exchange Bonds

The two big exchanges in New York City make a market for bonds as well as stocks. Most of these bonds (in jargon, "debentures") are the debts of large corporations. But the New York Bond Exchange also carries a few listings for bonds issued by foreign governments.

Trading in bonds is not a game recommended for casual investors. Bonds are contracts written by the borrower. And often these contracts, which spell out in detail the corporate borrower's obligations to the bond owners, are quite complicated.

For example, one has to know more than the creditworthiness of a company to judge the creditworthiness of its bonds. Some bonds are "junior" debt: in the event the company is unable to meet its obligations, the owners of such bonds must wait until other creditors are paid off.

Other bonds are "equipment trust certificates," in effect, mortgages on, say, a specific airplane or factory complex owned by the borrower. With equipment trusts, the security of your bond depends less on the credit of the borrower than on the market value of the equipment pledged as collateral.

Many bonds, moreover, contain "call" provisions which allow the borrower to buy back the bonds at a specified price long before maturity. Such provisions work entirely in the borrower's favor. If interest rates in the economy go down, the borrower can redeem the bonds and borrow the money elsewhere at a lower rate. But if interest rates rise, the borrower is under no obligation to redeem the bonds before the maturity. The lender is thus stuck with below-market interest.

The bottom line: Never buy a bond unless you know what you are buying. The only way to be sure what's in the bond contract is to read the prospectus published when the bond was first issued. Any broker worth his commission will be happy to supply you with a copy.

Column 1. A bond is identified by the company that issued it, the interest it pays, and the year in which it matures. Thus "Exxon 6½ 98" is shorthand for a bond issued by the Exxon Corporation that pays 6.5 percent interest ($65 a year) on the $1,000 face value of the bond and matures sometime in 1998. All this information is provided to identify the bond issue outstanding. "DetEd 9.15s00" is a Detroit Edison Corp. bond paying 9.15 percent interest ($91.50) annually that matures in the year 2000. Interest on most bonds is paid in semiannual installments. Thus owners of the DetEd9.15s00 expect $45.75 every six months.

The maturity date tells you the year in which the bond must be redeemed by the issuing company at the original $1,000 face value. It is possible—no, likely—that the bond contains a call provision giving the company the option to redeem the bond years earlier. The only way to find out is to read the bond prospectus or consult a research service that keeps track of bonds.

"CATS zr06-11" is not a corporate bond at all, but a "Certificate of Accrual on Treasury Securities." This is an obligation of a big bond dealer to pay the holder $1,000 on the maturity date. What makes the obligation special is that it is backed by a U.S. government bond of equal value. Notice the zr; that means this is a zero coupon bond paying no current interest. The profit to the investor is the difference between what he or she pays for the CATS today and their guaranteed value on redemption. This particular CATS has two dates listed, rather than just one. That means it may be redeemed as early as 2006 or as late as 2011.

The t in "Citicp 6.5s98t" means that the interest payment of this Citicorp bond floats—that is, it is adjusted periodically according to some formula that reflects movements in current interest rates. *The advantage of a floating rate security is that the price won't fluctuate very much as interest rates change*. The disadvantage is that you pay for the lower risk: floating-rate bonds pay lower interest than the fixed-rate bonds of equivalently credit-worthy borrowers.

Column 2. The current yield is the annual interest the company promises to pay, divided by the last price at which the bond was sold (see column 5).

All bonds are issued in $1,000 denominations. But, just to confuse things, bond prices are listed as a percentage of the $1,000 face value rather than in dollars. Thus the closing price of the Citicorp bond is 91⅛ percent of $1,000, or $911.25. To obtain the current yield of the Citicorp bond, divide the interest payment $65 by the closing price of $911.25. That equals 7.13. To save space in the listings, the figure is rounded to the nearest tenth—7.1.

There is no current yield for AshO (Ashland Oil); instead there is only a cv. The cv means the bond is convertible into a specified number of shares of stock in Ashland Oil.

It would be easy enough to calculate a current yield for the Ashland Oil convertible ($67.50 divided by $892.50 equals 7.6 percent). But the number is not printed in the listings because the price of convertible bonds is partially determined by the price of the stock and the terms of the conversion.

Column 3. The volume is the number of bonds that traded hands that day. For example, 26 of the Exxon bonds were traded.

Consider how small this figure is. Exxon is the

(TABLE 2)

EXCHANGE BONDS*

	1	2	3	4		5	6
		CUR					NET
	BONDS	YLD	VOL	HIGH	LOW	CLOSE	CHG
AshO	6¾ 14	cv	2	90	89	89¼	-¾
CATS	zr06-11	—	35	17	16¾	17	—
Citicp	6.5s98t	7.1	11	91⅛	91	91⅛	+⅛
DetEd	9.15s00	9.0	5	102	102	102	—
Exxon	6½ 98	6.8	26	95¾	95	95½	-¼

*Transaction information for illustration only.

largest oil company in the world. Yet just $26,000 worth of this bond issue traded on this day. Exxon does have other bonds outstanding, paying different interest rates and maturing at other dates. But even if you include them, the value of bonds traded daily is minuscule compared to the hundreds of millions of dollars worth of Exxon stock that changes hands each day.

The Exxon example is not unusual. Most bonds are purchased by big institutions—pension funds, insurance companies—and either held to maturity or sold in very large blocks in transactions off the exchange. Total trading on the New York Bond Exchange that day was less than $30 million. Compare that to total trading on the New York Stock Exchange, which exceeded $2 billion.

Low volumes matter to individual investors because they make corporate bonds relatively illiquid. If, for example, you tried to sell fifty Exxon bonds on a single day, you might end up receiving $10 or $20 less per bond than you anticipated.

Column 4. The highest and lowest prices at which bonds traded that day. Unless there is an *f* (for "flat") after the bond listing, buyers are also obliged to pay the seller any accrued but unpaid interest on the bond. The buyer gets the money back, of course, when the company makes its semiannual interest payment.

Column 5. The last price at which bonds were traded. There is generally no way of telling how many bonds traded at this closing price. We have no idea from the listings whether just one Exxon bond or 25 of the 26 bonds traded were sold for 95½. Of course, if the high and low price for the day were the same (as in the case of the Detroit Edison bonds), we can be sure that all the bonds sold at that single price.

Column 6. The change in the closing price from the previous day. For example, the Citicorp bond closed at 91⅛ ($911.25), up ⅛ from the previous close of 91 ($910).

With the exception of convertible issues, price movements in bonds generally reflect changes in interest rates in the economy. If interest rates go up, the prices of existing bonds must go down in order to make them as attractive to investors as newly issued bonds. If interest rates go down, bond prices rise.

The longer the remaining term of the bond, the more it will fluctuate in value. Thus investors tempted by the generally high yields on longer-term bonds must consider that they bear more risk.

Other footnotes you may occasionally find in the bond listings:

cf—Certificates. Most bonds are traded in "registered" form where all the information about ownership is kept in computers and there is no exchange of paper when the securities are traded. Bonds with certificates do it the old-fashioned way with the piece of paper as proof of ownership, much like the deed on real estate.

cld—The company has issued a notice that it will redeem the bond for cash, on terms specified in the original offering; bonds that have been called are worth the stipulated call price (typically the face value plus a few percent), but pay no interest.

dc—Deep discount: A bond selling for at least 20 percent less than its face value. This occurs because the bond pays much less than market-rate interest on a semiannual basis or simply because investors doubt that the issuer will be able to come up with the cash to meet its obligations.

ec—The bond's face value and interest payments are calculated in European Currency Units—an index of the value of most of the currencies of countries belonging to the European Common Market.

il—Traded in Italian lira.

kd—Traded in Danish kroner.

m—A matured bond that's worth its face value but pays no interest.

r—Registered: Ownership information is recorded and maintained by the issuer. Convenient for everyone but cocaine dealers and tax evaders.

wd—When distributed: The bond has yet to be distributed to buyers, but is being offered for sale on the basis of the promised distribution.

ww—A bond that comes with warrants to buy the company stock at a predetermined price.

zw—Without warrants: The bond was probably initially issued with warrants to buy shares of the company stock, but is being offered for sale without the warrants.

vi—The bond issuer is in bankruptcy.

U.S. Treasury Bonds
and Notes

U.S. Treasury bonds are government debts that mature ten years or more from their date of issue. U.S. Treasury notes mature in more than one year and less than ten from their issue date. Both pay interest twice a year and are backed by the ultimate source of dollar-denominated credit, the U.S. Government. *Uncle Sam won't guarantee that the money will be worth much, but he certainly can guarantee that owners of Treasury bonds and notes will be paid every penny they are owed, on time.*

Treasury bonds and notes are initially sold at auctions. Afterwards they are traded "over the counter" by hundreds of dealers linked together by a computer system. Unlike the over-the-counter market for stocks, this market is very large, very liquid, and very efficient. Billions of dollars' worth of government securities change hands every day, usually in blocks of a million dollars' worth or more. Individual investors can buy or sell in this market through commercial banks and securities brokers. Commissions are relatively low, and for those in a hurry, the proceeds of a sale can be made available in cash the next business day.

Column 1. The annual interest, paid in semiannual checks. Treasury bonds and notes are issued in $1,000 denominations. So the 7 percent security in the first row of the table pays $70 a year in two installments of $35. Note how much the interest rate varies from security to security. That's because some were issued in the late 1970s and early 1980s paying rates as high as 15 percent.

Column 2. The year in which the bond matures and the government is obligated to pay back the $1,000 face value. This sample list is, of course, quite abbreviated. Over 200 separate issues of bonds and notes are traded each day, with the figures listed in order of the maturity date.

Notice the 7⅝ percent issue, with what appears to be a double maturity date (02-07). That means the bond must be redeemed at face value by Feb. 2007, but the government has the option of redeeming it any time after Feb. 2002. The government's decision on when to redeem the bond will depend on interest rates in 2002 and beyond. If Uncle Sam can refinance the debt at a lower rate, the bond will probably be called.

(TABLE 3)

TREASURY BONDS AND NOTES*

1	2	3	4	5	6
	MATURITY				ASK
RATE	MO/YR	BID	ASKED	CHG	YLD
7	Sept96n	99:25	99:27	+3	7.04
8¾	Oct97n	106:15	106:17	+2	7.30
13%	Aug01	137:31	138:03	—	7.62
7⅞	Feb02-07	98:25	98:25	+1	7.75
8⅛	May21	100:20	100:22	+4	8.06

*Transaction information for illustration only.

An *n* following the month means the security is a note, originally issued to mature in less than ten years. The distinction means little to investors in the secondary Treasury market.

Column 3. The "Bid" is the highest price dealers were willing to pay at the close of the trading day. The number is a percentage of the $1,000 face value. Confusingly, the numbers after the colon are not 100ths of a percent, but 32nds. So the bid of 99:25 on the first security means that dealers will pay 99 and 25/32nds of the $1,000 face value of the note, or $997.81. Likewise, the 137:31 bid on the 13⅜ bond of August 2001 is equal to $1,379.70. Practice the arithmetic a little with a pocket calculator; you'll find it isn't as hard as it looks.

Column 4. The "Asked" figure is the lowest price at which dealers were willing to sell the security at the end of the trading day. The difference between the bid and asked price is typically quite small; 4 represents only $1.25. That narrow range is an indication of just how deep and liquid the government bond market is. Occasionally, though, the gap balloons to as much as $10 on less heavily traded issues, proving the government bond market is a good market, but not a perfect one.

Column 5. The "Change" is the difference between the closing bid that day and the closing bid the previous day. Day-to-day movements in bond prices are typically small relative to stocks. Don't be fooled, though; this is hardly a sedate market. For the big traders who buy hundreds of millions' worth of securities daily with borrowed funds, an unanticipated movement of a few 32nds can mean the loss of enormous sums.

Column 6. The "Ask Yield" is the yield to maturity, the annualized profit that an investor would make by buying the security at the asked price and holding it until the government returns the $1,000 principle. Unlike the bid and asked figures, the numbers after the period are 100ths. So 8.06 means what it says.

Note that "yield to maturity" is crucially different from the "current yield" in the listings for corporate bonds. It includes both the annual interest earnings and any gain or loss in capital value between the purchase date and the date of redemption.

Consider, for example, the 13⅜ bond of August 2001. Its current yield for a new purchaser is about 9.6 percent—far more than the 7.62 percent listed in the yield column. But part of the profit from the $133.75 annual interest will go to offset the difference between what an investor would pay for the bond today ($1,389.40) and the $1,000 the government will return in August 2001. It takes a fancy pocket calculator to calculate bond yields. Happily, they are listed in the paper.

U.S. Treasury Strips

Zero-coupon bonds—bonds that pay all their accumulated interest at maturity—are much in demand for a variety of reasons. Big investors like them because their value changes so rapidly in response to changes in interest rates in the economy. And many small investors like them because they know exactly how much money (interest and principal) they will end up with after one or two or twenty years.

So some very clever Wall Street types have created zero-coupon bonds by taking apart standard U.S. Treasury securities and putting them back together in a slightly different form. Here's how it works.

Consider an ordinary 8 percent, 20-year U.S. Treasury bond. It consists of the Treasury's promise to pay $40 every six months (half of the $80 annual interest), plus $1,000 at the end of the twentieth year. If you bought, say, 25 of them, Uncle Sam would owe you $1,000 every six months, plus $25,000 at the end of 20 years. Each of these $1,000 promises-to-pay could thus be "stripped" off the package of 25 bonds and resold to investors as zero-coupon bonds maturing sequentially every six months. Meanwhile, the $25,000 payment due in 20 years could be sold as 25 separate zero-coupon bonds with face values of $1,000 that matured in 20 years.

Once you know how to read the tables for Treasury notes and bonds, interpreting the tables for U.S. Treasury Strips is a snap.

(TABLE 4)

U.S. TREASURY STRIPS*

1	2	3		4	5
MAT	TYPE	BID	ASKED	CHG.	ASK YIELD
Jul 02	np	73:17	73:20	+6	6:11
Nov 09	bp	42:27	43:00	+8	6:66
Aug 22	ci	17:28	18:00	+7	6:80

*Transaction information for illustration only.

Column 1. The month and year in which the Treasury will pay the bond owner the $1,000 face value. Unlike ordinary Treasury bonds, there is no face-value interest rate cited because there is no interest paid directly by the

Treasury. The interest on zero-coupon bonds is implicit—the difference between what you pay and what you get at maturity.

Column 2. The symbol np stands for principle from a note, showing that this particular Treasury strip was once part of a Treasury note. The symbol bp means principle from a Treasury bond, while the symbol ci means the payout consists of coupon interest from a number of different bonds or notes. Now that you've learned this information, relax and forget it. No matter how it is assembled, a Treasury strip is a promise to pay the owner $1,000 on the assigned maturity date.

Column 3. The bid and asked notation is identical to that of ordinary Treasury bonds. The bid price on the August 2022 strip, 17:28, translates as $170 + ^{28}\!/_{32}$ of $10, for a total of $178.75.

Column 4. The change from the previous day's closing price, in 32nds of $10. Thus the November 2009 strip rose by $^8\!/_{32}$ of $10, or $2.50.

Column 5. The yield to maturity an investor, who paid the asking price, would get if she held the strip to maturity. In other words, an investor who paid 18:00 (that is $180) today for the August 2022 strip and held it to 2022 would earn 6.80% on her money.

Government Agency Bonds

Dealers in U.S. Treasury securities also buy and sell securities issued by two dozen other U.S. government agencies, non-profit corporations chartered by Congress, and international development agencies supported by governments. Some newspapers only list the more popular agency securities daily and provide a more comprehensive listing on Sundays.

The tables are usually grouped after Treasury bonds and notes. Notations for all bonds are identical: we illustrate them with listings from the Federal Home Loan Bank. Most agency bonds are relatively safe because they are backed by substantial assets. *Keep in mind, though, that not all bonds with the word "federal" in their names are guaranteed by the U.S. Treasury. Nor are all such securities exempt from state and local taxes.* Remember, too, that while agency bonds pay higher interest rates than Treasury issues, the market is considerably thinner.

Should you need to sell some in a hurry, you may get back less than you expected.

(TABLE 5)

AGENCY BONDS*

FEDERAL HOME LOAN BANK

RATE	MAT	BID	ASKED	YIELD
9.50	2-04	117:08	117:04	6.41
6.95	2-06	98:24	99:00	7.10
7.18	1-11†	98:04	98:12	7.37

*Transaction information for illustration only.
Note: A dagger (†) after the maturity date shows that the bond is callable before maturity.

Column 1. The annual interest rate on the security. With few exceptions, interest is paid in two semiannual installments.

Column 2. The month and year the security matures. With very few exceptions, agency securities contain no "call" provision. That means the issuing agency does not have the right to redeem the bond for the original issue price before the maturity date.

Column 3. The price dealers were willing to pay at the close at the trading day. Prices are quoted like Treasury bonds and notes. The number before the colon is a percentage, while the number after is 32nds of a percent. With Agency bonds selling in units of $1,000, it is easy to translate the percentage into a dollar figure. A bid of, say, 99:04 on a security selling for $1,000 is equal to 99 and ½nds of $1,000, or $991.25.

But while some agency bonds are issued in $1,000 multiples, others come in multiples of $5,000, $10,000, $25,000, or even $100,000. Here is an abbreviated list:

AGENCY	MINIMUM	GOVT. GUARANTEED?
Asian Development Bank	$ 1,000	no
Export-Import Bank	$ 5,000	yes
Federal Farm Credit	$ 1,000	no
Federal Home Loan Bank	$10,000	no
Federal National Mortgage Assn	$10,000	no
Govt National Mortgage Assn	$ 5,000	yes
World Bank	$ 1,000	no

Column 4. The price at which dealers were willing to sell, again quoted as a percentage of issue price. Should you buy an agency bond, you'll also have to figure in any accrued but unpaid interest since the last semiannual installment.

Column 5. The yield to maturity. That's the annualized return you would get if you bought the security for the asked price and held it to maturity. For securities selling below 100, this return consists of the semiannual interest, plus the gain when the agency redeems the bond for face value. For securities selling above 100, the profit is the interest, less the capital loss when the security is redeemed.

Treasury Bills

Treasury bills (T-bills) are government securities that mature in one year or less. T-bills are initially sold in maturities of 91 days, three months, six months, nine months, and one year and in minimum denominations of $10,000. You can buy newly issued T-bills direct from the Federal Reserve. Or you can buy them in the secondary, "over-the-counter" government securities market. Commercial banks and securities brokers are happy to do the paper work for a small commission.

Reading the newspaper tables requires a little understanding of how T-bills differ from longer-term government bonds and notes. Bonds and notes pay interest twice a year. T-bills, by contrast, pay interest only indirectly through the device of the "discount." The buyer initially pays less than the $10,000 face amount of the bill—perhaps, $9,700. When the bill expires, the government returns the $10,000 face amount. The $300 difference, or discount, is the interest earned by the investor.

(TABLE 6)					
TREASURY BILLS*					
1		2	3	4	5
	DAYS TO				
MATURITY	MATURITY	BID	ASKED	CHG	ASK YLD
Jan 02 '97	3	3.55	3.51	+0.03	3.56
May 15 '97	136	5.07	5.05	+0.04	5.22
Jan 08 '98	374	5.21	5.19	—	5.48
*Transaction information for illustration only.					

Column 1. The month, day, and year on which the bill matures and the Treasury pays back the principle. The listing now includes the number of days to maturity, a figure that helps the heavy-duty financial types who use Treasury bills to park corporate cash for brief periods to plan more easily.

Column 2. It looks like an interest rate, printed out to two decimal places. But it's really a backhanded way of stating the price that dealers were willing to pay for the security at the close of the trading day.

Here's how to think about it: Dealers figure how much

they are willing to pay for a bill in dollars and cents. Then they divide the discount (the difference between what the dealer is willing to pay and the $10,000 face value) by the face value and figure the annualized yield to maturity.

Confused? Try it with numbers: A dealer says he will pay $9,700 for a bill that will mature to its $10,000 face value in four months. He then divides the discount of $300 ($10,000 minus $9,700) by the $10,000 face value. $300 divided by $10,000 equals 3 percent for one-third of a year. On an annualized basis, the interest is three times that much, or 9 percent. So a dealer who bids "9.00" for a bill due to mature in four months is really offering to pay $9,700 for the bill.

Column 3. This "asked" figure works like the bid. It is a weird way of stating the price at which dealers are willing to sell the security at the close of the trading day. Another example might help:

Say a dealer is willing to sell a bill due to mature in four months for $9,702. The discount is $298 ($10,000 minus $9,702). Dividing the $298 discount by the $10,000 face value, we get 2.98 percent. On an annualized basis, that equals 3 times 2.98, or 8.94 percent. So a dealer who asks "8.94" for a bill due to mature in four months is really offering to sell the bill for $9,702.

Two additional thoughts: No. 1, *the "asked" number is always smaller than the "bid." That may not look right, but it is.* The more you pay for a Treasury bill, the lower the interest return will be. No. 2, *the difference between the bid and the asked price for Treasury bills is some-*

times only pennies. Dealers can still make big money, though, because they trade tens of thousands of bills every day.

Column 5. The yield is the actual annualized yield that an investor would receive if he or she paid the price the dealers are asking and then held the bill to maturity. For investors, it's the one that really counts.

When bid and asked figures are calculated, the discount is divided by the $10,000 face. That was very convenient for the clerks who had to do the arithmetic quickly before the invention of electronic calculators. But the resulting number always underestimates the true return, because the investor never has to plunk down the full $10,000.

For example, if the asking figure on a one-year T-bill is "8.00," the dealers are offering to sell the T-bill for $800 less than $10,000, or $9,200. The investor's yield on the $9,200 is $800 divided by $9,200, or 8.70 percent.

Still confused? Ignore everything reported in the tables except the yield. That allows you to compare the return on T-bills with the return on other investments.

Tax-Exempt Bonds

Tax-exempt bonds are the debts of state and local governments, as well as public agencies that invest in housing, irrigation, electric power generation, toll roads, and practically anything else that has some public purpose. As the name implies, the interest income (but not capital gain when the bonds are sold) is free from Federal tax. Most states also exempt the interest income on municipal bonds issued within their own borders. Note, however, that the exemption only works within-state: Pennsylvania residents must pay Pennsylvania tax on bonds issued in Michigan.

Tax-exempts are divided into two broad categories: "general obligation" bonds backed by the taxing power of a government, and "revenue" bonds backed by a specific stream of income such as tolls, water charges, and sports stadium revenues. Another significant distinction is the "private activity" bond whose interest is exempt from Federal taxes, but may still change tax liability because it is a so-called "preference item" in calculating the Federal alternative minimum tax. If you think this may matter to you, consult an accountant.

In recent years, most tax-exempts have been in the revenue category. And with a few exceptions, the bonds listed in daily newspapers are revenue bonds.

(TABLE 7)					
TAX-EXEMPT BONDS*					
1	2	3	4	5	6
				BID	
ISSUE	COUPON	MAT	PRICE	CHG	YLD
Broward					
Co Fla	5.625	09-01-28	99¼	+⅛	5.67
Ca Var					
Pur Genl					
Obl	5.250	06-01-21	95½	+¼	5.58
MTA NY	5.250	04-01-26	94⅞	+¼	5.61

*Transaction information for illustration only.

Column 1. The name of the issuing authority. Literally thousands of different entities have tax-exempt bonds outstanding. Only about 75, though, are traded actively enough to rate a listing in the paper. The listings can be quite useful, even if you own (or are considering owning) a different tax-exempt bond, since most issues track the heavily traded ones here.

Two of the three bonds in this list are "general obligation" bonds. The third, issued by the Metropolitan Transit Authority of New York, is backed by transit revenues.

Column 2. The annual percentage interest paid by the bond. This payment—actually two semiannual payments—is called the "coupon" because some bonds actually have interest coupons that must be clipped and redeemed through banks or securities brokers. Since 1983 all new bonds have been issued in "registered" form; meaning that the money is paid electronically or by check to the owner of record. This has spoiled a good game—namely, hiding untaxed profits in tax-exempt bonds, whose interest is not reported to Uncle Sam.

Column 3. The date the bonds mature. Most tax-exempts have call provisions that make it extremely likely the bonds will be redeemed before the maturity date.

Column 4. The closing price, quoted as a percentage of the face value, that dealers are willing to pay for large lots of bonds (typically a few hundred thousand dollars' worth). Thus a major seller of the Broward County issue (most likely a bank) could expect to get $992.50 per bond. Someone selling, say 10 bonds, through a broker would more likely get something on the order of $985 per bond.

Buyers of tax-exempts are obliged to pay any interest that has been accrued since the last semiannual payment. The buyers get their money back when the next interest payment is made.

Column 5. The change in price from the previous day's close, again expressed as a percentage of $1,000. The Broward County bonds rose $1.25.

Column 6. The yield if the bonds were purchased at the day's closing price and held to maturity. The actual yield could be quite a bit less on bonds purchased above their face value and called well before maturity.

The yield on tax-exempt bonds is substantially lower than the yield on taxable bonds of equivalent safety and maturity. Buyers, in essence, pay for the privilege of avoiding taxable interest—which implies that investors in low tax brackets can often do better buying taxable bonds.

Mutual Funds

Mutual funds are companies that sell shares to the public, then invest the proceeds in stocks, bonds, and other securities. Some are quite specialized, investing in just one industry (telecommunications), one country (Russia), or one size of company (stocks with outstanding shares worth less than $100 million). More typically, mutual funds diversify their holdings across many industries and, recently, many nations.

An "open-end" mutual fund is not your average corporation. Ordinary, publicly owned corporations infrequently issue new shares of stock in order to raise capital. If you want to own shares, you buy them from someone who already owns a piece of the company. An open-end mutual fund, by contrast, has no fixed number of shares. The fund grows when investors buy new shares directly from the fund or from a sales agent working on commission—typically a brokerage house such as Merrill Lynch.

Each share represents proportional ownership of the underlying assets of the mutual fund. In a sense it is a slice of the pie that consists of a portfolio of securities. When investors choose to sell their shares, they sell them back to the fund under terms set in the original sales contract. The redemption value is determined by the value of the mutual fund's assets.

The owners of the mutual fund—typically an investment company such as Fidelity or Vanguard—make a profit by taking a percentage of the assets as a fee each year. Some also charge fees to buy or redeem shares.

In order to avoid paying separate income taxes as corporations, mutual funds are legally obliged to pay out all their earnings to the shareowners. Most funds allow investors to reinvest their earnings automatically. But, reinvested or not, shareowners are liable for income taxes on all the fund's profit distributions during the calendar year. Never buy a fund without finding out what tax liability comes with ownership.

Column 1. The net asset value per share, as calculated by the fund. The figure represents the market value of one share's worth of the underlying security at the close of the previous business day. For example, behind every share of Vangaurd's Windsor Fund are stocks worth $16.48.

Column 2. The change in value per share (in dollars) from the beginning of the trading day to the end.

(TABLE 8)

MUTUAL FUNDS*

1	2	3	4	5	6	7			8	9
NAV	NET CHG	FUND NAME	INV OBJ	YTD %RET	4WK %RET	TOTAL RETURN 1YR	3YR-R	5YR-R	MAX INIT CHRG	EXP RATIO
VANGUARD										
10.41	+0.03	GNMA	MG	+5.4	+1.3	5.9B	6.9A	6.7 A	0.00	0.29
16.48	- 0.06	Wndsr	GI	26.4	- 1.2	27.6A	19.4B	18.6A	0.00	0.45

*Transaction information for illustration only.

Column 3. Funds are listed in groups under the name of the investment company that manages them—in this case, the Vanguard Group. It's not always obvious what the abbreviations stand for (GNMA is Vanguard's fund that invests in government-insured mortgage securities). However, once you own a fund, you know what to look for. The names of individual funds are sometimes followed by footnotes in lower-case letters. These can vary a bit from listing to listing. But here's a brief, if less than comprehensive, scorecard:

e—Ex-distribution, meaning a new buyer is not entitled to a cash or share distribution that has been declared but not yet paid to fund owners.

f—The previous day's net asset value quotation, presumably because today's was not available.

g—Footnotes x and s apply (go figure . . .)

i—Comparisons with other funds can be misleading because costs are calculated in an unusual way.

j—Footnotes e and s apply.

k—Recalculated using more up-to-date (but not generally available) data.

p—Distribution costs included.

r—A fee for redeeming shares may be charged.

s—A dividend in the form of stock has recently been given to shareowners.

t—Footnotes p and r apply.

v—Footnotes x and e apply.

x—Ex-dividend, meaning a new buyer is not entitled

to a recent dividend that has been declared but not yet paid to fund owners.

z—Footnotes x, e, and s all apply.

Column 4. The investment strategy of the fund, as stated in the fund's formal prospectus. Note that once in operation, funds typically give themselves considerable discretion to shift strategies. This makes the classifications of limited value: let the buyer beware.

Stock funds:

CP—Capital appreciation. The primary goal is rapid growth in asset value. These funds often trade their assets frequently and are higher risk investments because they are likely to record higher-than-average losses when the overall value of the market is falling.

GR—Growth. Focuses on companies with higher than average growth in earnings and revenues.

GI—Growth and Income. Mixes the objectives of high dividends and price increases.

EI—Equity Income. Favors stocks that pay high dividends. These stocks are less risky, but offer less potential for rapid appreciation.

SC—Small Company. Focuses on smaller companies, typically ones that pay low dividends but may grow rapidly.

MC—MidCap. Focuses on middle-size companies that aren't giant name-brands like IBM, but don't qualify as small.

SE—Sector. Focuses on stocks within a single industry category. Among the categories: Health Care/Biotechnology, Environmental, Natural Resources, Regulated Utilities, High Technology, Real Estate, Precious Metals, Financial Services.

GL—Global Stock. Diversifies to stocks from many countries, which may include the United States.

IL—International Stock. Stocks from outside the United States. Among the categories are regions (Europe, Pacific, Japan, Latin America, Canada), less developed countries called emerging markets, and small companies.

Taxable Bond Funds:

SB—Short-Term. Very rapidly maturing, very secure debt of corporations. As a practical matter, equivalent to a money market fund.

SG—Short-Term U.S. Government. Very rapidly maturing debt issued or guaranteed by the U.S. government.

IB—Intermediate Term Bonds. High-quality debt that matures in less than 10 years. Riskier than short-term funds but less risky than funds investing in bonds with long maturities.

IG—Intermediate U.S. government. U.S. government debt maturing in less than 10 years.

AB—High-Quality debt of corporations with long average maturity.

LG—Long-term debt of the U.S. government.

GT—General Taxable. Invests in bonds of various terms and various quality.

HC—High Yield. Bonds that pay high interest because there is greater-than-average risk of default. Called "junk bonds" in the 1980s.

MG—Mortgage. Invests in securities that consist of mortgages, typically home mortgages.

WB—World. Debts of foreign corporations and governments.

Tax-Exempt Bond Funds:

SM—Short-Term Municipal Bonds. Very rapidly maturing debt of towns, states, and public authorities whose interest payments are not taxed by the Feds.

IM—Intermediate Munis. Intermediate term "municipal" bonds, a term that has become shorthand for any Federally tax-exempt bond.

GM—General Municipal. May invest in virtually any tax-exempt bond.

SS—Single State Munis. Invest in munis from a single state. Created for the convenience of state residents, who don't pay state or Federal taxes on the interest. Not that, say, a California fund is a bad deal for a New York resident just because New York will tax the interest.

HM—High Yield Municipal. Invests in munis that pay high interest because there is fear the payments won't be made.

NM—Insured Municipal. Invests only in bonds whose timely payment of interest and return to principle is insured by a confederation of private insurance companies.

MP—Multipurpose. Fund that invests in stocks and hybrid securities as well as bonds.

Column 5. The fund's percentage return for the current year to date, including both dividends and capital appreciation. To arrive at the figure, it is assumed that all fund dividends are invested in more shares.

Column 6. The fund's percentage return for the last four weeks.

Column 7. The fund's percentage return over the past 12 months, three years, and five years, assuming all fund dividends are reinvested. The three- and five-year figures are in annual terms. Thus in the example, the Windsor fund averaged a 19.4 percent annual return over the previous three years. Think of it as the equivalent of compound interest. In many cases, longer-term total returns are unavailable (NA) because the fund hasn't existed for very long. By the same token, funds that are unsuccessful at attracting or keeping investors are often liquidated.

The capital letters after the total return figures are ranking of past performance, as compared to other funds in the same category. The five categories run A (top fifth) through E (bottom fifth). Note that past performance is not much of an indicator of future performance. Also note that relatively low total returns can produce high rankings if the category of investment didn't do very well. As per the example, Vanguard's GNMA fund produced only modest returns but still ranked high because mortgage securities generally didn't do very well.

Column 8. Maximum initial sales charge. Vanguard funds are "no-load" funds that do not subtract a sales fee from the initial investment. But initial sales charges can run as high as 5.75 percent, and there is little if any relationship between the charges and the performance of the fund itself. Many funds charge no load, but do extract a fee for redemption.

Column 9. Expense ratio. Annual expenses of the fund, shown as a percentage of the fund's assets. These expenses include both management fees and marketing costs. Vangaurd funds have relatively low expense ratios. The funds that advertise heavily, trade securities frequently, and pay their managers well may have expense ratios as high as 2 or 3 percent. Sometimes the expenses pay off in the form of high, after-expense returns for investors. All too often, though, they don't.

Money Market Mutual Funds

Money market funds are mutual funds that invest in very safe, very liquid short-term securities, such as U.S. Treasury bills, bank certificates of deposit, and secured loans to large corporations. Investors' income consists of the interest earned, less charges by the sponsoring investment firm. Some money market funds are available only to specific groups—for example, customers of a securities broker or members of non-profit groups such as the American Association of Retired Persons. Others cater only to the wealthy, requiring a minimum initial investment as high as $20,000. But most are delighted to do business with people willing to invest a minimum of $1,000 to $2,500.

Money market funds are, for most practical purposes, interchangeable with money market accounts at banks.

Like banks, funds try to discourage heavy use of the checking privilege; most funds manage this by placing a $250 or $500 minimum on the size of checks that can be written. But unlike bank accounts, money market funds are not insured by the Federal Government. They are still very safe, however, because shares in a money market fund are specific ownership claims on very secure assets.

Column 1. The name of the fund. Roughly two hundred are listed weekly in major newspapers.

The letter *f* indicates that the figures are from the day previous to the standard reporting day. The letter *c:* the fund invests primarily in municipal bonds, so the return to investors is largely exempt from federal tax. The letter *b:* the yield shown is the yield earned by the average size account. Smaller accounts earned less, larger accounts more. This usually arises because the fund charges a fixed monthly minimum—say $3—to maintain the account. If an account is very small, the minimum may eat up a good portion of the earnings.

Slightly different methods are used to calculate the current interest return on funds. The letter *a* indicates that a fund includes capital gains and losses in the computation of yield, as well as actual interest payments on the securities in its portfolio. This can be important; if interest rates in the economy go up or down rapidly, the fund will incur capital losses or gains, and the reported yield will be distorted by as much as a full percentage point for a brief period. *Moral: If you happen to be attracted to a fund that includes capital changes in its reported yields, be sure to compare its record over several weeks before investing.*

Column 2. The number of days until the average security in the fund's portfolio matures. The longer the average maturity, the greater the risk that the income earned by the fund will include capital losses or gains. That's why no money market fund allows its portfolio maturity to become very long; three months is exceptional. So the risk of losing more than a fraction of a percent of assets is very small, even for the funds with the longest average maturity.

Column 3. The yield for the previous seven days, at an annualized rate, earned by investors. When comparing these rates with rates on longer-term savings such as bank certificates, remember to make allowances for compounding. A money market fund credits interest to your account every day. So you earn interest on your accumulating interest. That can add a few tenth's of a percent annually to your earnings that are not accounted for in the tables.

Money markets investing in the same types of securities pay roughly equivalent rates of return. Why, then, do the average yields in the listing vary from 3 to 5 percent?

The lower rates are for funds that invest entirely in the tax-exempt debt of government authorities, and are thus themselves exempt from Federal income tax. Tax-exempt funds may not deliver superior after-tax returns for investors: it all depends on their tax brackets. For example, a 3.00 percent return, tax-free, is equivalent to 4.35 percent for an investor in the 31 percent Federal bracket. And should one reside in a high-tax state such as California, the effective return may be even higher if the money market fund invests entirely in tax-exempt obligations from California.

There are other reasons, though, why yields differ between funds. One is expenses: some funds, notably those that accept small initial deposits, generally charge more for their services. Another is safety: funds that invest entirely in government securities pay a bit less and are a bit more secure than funds that buy the obligations of banks and other financial institutions. But the difference in both safety and yield is very modest, indeed.

(TABLE 9)

MONEY MARKET MUTUAL FUNDS*

1 NAME	2 AVERAGE MATY	3 7 DAY YIELD
AARP HQ	46	5.42
BenhmPrime	60	4.99
EvgrTreasA	39	4.78
Dela TaxFrA	44	3.13
Benhm NatTF	40	3.37
Salomon NY	30	3.01

*Transaction information for illustration only.

Closed-End Bond Funds and Publicly Traded Mutual Funds

Most mutual funds are "open-ended": You buy shares from the sponsoring investment company that invests the proceeds in common stocks, bonds, precious metals, etc. Should you want to sell the shares, the investment company buys them back for the underlying value of the assets the shares represent, less any redemption fees.

But there is another, lesser known type of mutual fund which is "closed-ended." These funds sell a fixed number of shares to the public. After the initial public offering, those who want to invest must buy shares from the other owners, much the way investors buy shares of IBM or General Motors. By the same token, the only way to sell shares in a closed-end fund is to find someone who wants to buy them.

Closed-end funds are listed in two separate newspaper columns: "Closed-end Funds," consisting of funds that invest primarily in bonds, and "Publicly Traded Funds," which invest in common stocks and securities convertible into common stock.

Buying and selling shares in either category is easy, for there are established markets for fund shares. Some are listed on the New York and American stock exchanges. Others are sold "over the counter" by brokers linked by computer. The heavily traded closed-end funds are listed in daily newspapers along with ordinary corporate stocks. A more complete listing, with extra information, is printed weekly.

Column 1. The name of the fund. Information on about thirty funds is available on a weekly basis. Some of these funds are diversified common stock funds that buy stocks for growth potential and dividends. Most follow some specialized investment strategy. For example, the Korea Fund invests only in Korean stocks.

Column 2. The stock exchange on which the closed-end shares are regularly traded. N = New York, A = American, O = NASDAQ, M = Midwest, T = Toronto

Column 3. The net asset value per share of the underlying assets. For example, a 30 million share fund with assets that could be sold for $300 million would have a net asset value of $10.

Some relevant footnotes:

a—Ex-dividend. The shares are traded without any claim on the latest declared dividend.

b—Fully diluted. The net asset value accounts for any claims by owners of rights, warrants, and other conversion options.

c—As of Thursday's (as opposed to Friday's) close.

d—As of Wednesday's close.

e—As of Tuesday's close.

f—A rights offering, which may dilute the net asset value, is in progress.

g—A rights offering has been announced.

i—The stock has recently split.

j—A recent rights offering has expired, but the net asset value may not account for the expiration.

v—Converted at the commercial exchange rate between dollars and South African rand.

y—Traded in Canadian dollars.

Column 4. Where shares are traded on an exchange, the figures published over the weekend are for the Friday close. Remember that closed-end shares must be purchased through securities brokers, and thus you pay a commission. On the other hand, there is no "load" or sales charge, which is often exacted on purchases of open-end funds. Transaction fees are generally higher for funds traded "over the counter."

Column 5. The percentage difference between the market price and the net asset value. Note that two out of four of the funds in our sample listing are trading below net asset value. To put it bluntly, if the funds were liquidated and the cash delivered to the fund owners, they would come out ahead.

Why haven't they been liquidated? Fund managers hope that, given time, the market will recognize their genius and the gap will close. Cynics say the fund managers are putting their own interests ahead of the shareholders. After all, if the fund were liquidated there would be no more fat salaries and no more poached salmon and Chablis for lunch at the fund's expense.

Funds trading well below net asset value are often an interesting speculation because they deliver more bang for a buck. In the case of Adams Express, a $20,000 investment gives the owner a theoretical claim on $24,090 worth of stock. Funds selling at large discounts are occasionally taken over by large investors and then liquidated—at a profit to small investors who are along for the ride.

Some funds, of course, trade above net asset value. That's because the market values the managers' expertise in picking stocks. Or, in the case of funds that buy stocks in emerging markets such as India or Russia, there may be no other practical way to buy into the action.

(TABLE 10)

CLOSED-END FUNDS*

	1	2	3	4	5
	FUND NAME	STOCK EXCHANGE	NAV	MARKET PRICE	PERCENT DIFF
	Adams Express	N	24.09	20	-16.97
	TempEmMarkt	Na	17.44	18¾	+7.51
	QstValCap	N	40.17	35¾	-11.00
	DreyMun	A	9.70	9⅞	+1.80

*Transaction information for illustration only.

69

Stock Options

Stock options are the right to buy or sell shares of common stock for some agreed-upon price and time period. For example, I might sell you the option to purchase 100 shares of IBM stock for $150 a share any time in the next three months. Options trading on organized markets is anonymous. Brokers match buyers and sellers, just as they do on stock exchanges. Once the options agreement is made, however, it becomes a contract between the exchange and the investors. *Thus the purchaser of an option never need worry whether or not the seller will be willing or able to honor his commitment.*

The reasons for trading options vary. Conservative investors use options to reduce risk and raise their expected return by selling an option to buy stock they already own. Other investors buy options as an alternative to buying the underlying stock. That generally gives an investor more bang for the buck—bigger profits when the stock rises and, alas, bigger losses when the stock falls. Still others use option strategies as an alternative to selling "short" the underlying stock. They win if the stock falls in value.

As this is being written, options on over 200 stocks were available on the American, New York, Pacific, and Philadelphia exchanges as well as the Chicago Board of Trade. Options trading in the 100 most active stocks sold over the counter is set to begin soon. Listings for all the markets, including the proposed options for over-the-counter stocks, are identical.

Column 1. AMD is a major manufacturer of computer memory chips that from time to time attempts to wrestle some of the business for computer microprocessors from Intel. Options are available on the most heavily traded stocks and, in particular, the ones that have a track record for price volatility. The price listed below the option name is the closing stock price—very important information in pricing options.

Column 2. The strike price is the price at which the owner of the option has the right to buy (call) or to sell (put) the underlying stock.

Notice that AMD options are trading at four different strike prices. The range, $15 to $30 a share, reflects an estimate made by exchange officials of where investors expect the stock to end up in the coming months. The exchanges aim to please: where there is customer interest, strike prices are set in increments of $2.50 rather than $5.

(TABLE 11)

LISTED OPTION QUOTATIONS*

1	2	3	4		5	
			CALL		PUT	
OPTION	STRIKE	EXPIRES	VOL	LAST	VOL	LAST
AMD	15	Jan	200	12⅜	—	—
27⅞	25	Jan	688	3¼	158	¼
27⅞	27½	Jan	174	1⅝	150	⅞
27⅞	30	Apr	139	2⅝	—	—
27⅞	30	Jul	132	3⅝	—	—

LEAPS—LONG-TERM OPTIONS*

27⅞	15	JAN 98	104	13⅞	—	—
27⅞	30	JAN 98	95	5¾	2	5

*Transaction information for illustration only.

New strike prices are added as the stock price approaches the high or low end of the range.

Column 3. Owners of options have until the end of trading on the third Friday of the month listed to exercise an option. The longer the option, of course, the more it is worth. Note that trading is now possible in longer-term options known as "Leaps," whose expiration dates are as much as two years from the date the option is first traded.

Column 4. A call is an option to buy at a fixed price. Thus, at the end of this trading day, someone paid $3.25 for the option to buy a share of AMD stock for $25 before the third Friday in January. Options are very handy for speculators who want the biggest bang for a buck. Betting that AMD will go up by purchasing the stock requires an investment of $27.88 on this day. The same bet (for a limited time) could be made by purchasing a call option for just $3.25. But remember, financial leverage works both ways with call options. A modest decline in the price of the underlying stock will have a devastating impact on the value of the option.

A stock that is selling above the strike price (here $25) is "in the money." According to the listing, 688 "Jan 25 contracts" were traded this day (with contracts, the smallest unit traded is an option on 100 shares). So at the close of trading, buyers were paying $325 for Jan 25 contracts.

Column 5. A put is an option to sell at a fixed price. For most stocks at most times, puts are less heavily traded than calls. And with thin trading, the prices of options may be very volatile.

On this day, it seems, someone purchased two Jan 98 contracts to sell AMD stock at 30. Since they paid $5 per share for the privilege, they are apparently betting that AMD shares will fall below $25 per share. Puts can be used for speculation. Or, just as likely, for hedging. Suppose you already own AMD and want to guard against losses if the stock falls in price. Purchasing a put accomplishes this goal without forcing the investor to sell the stock.

Stock Index Options

A stock index option is a bet on the direction and size of a change of a stock index. Most of the indexes used are broad gauges of stock values. But options are also written on specialized indexes, such as the computer technology index, the transportation stock index, and the oil stock index.

Trading in index options is one of the fastest ways to make money on Wall Street. Unfortunately, index option trading is also one of the fastest ways to lose money. This casino-like quality has made index options immensely popular with speculators who want to maximize their bang for a buck. Institutional buyers also find them useful as tools in elaborate hedging and arbitrage strategies. Virtually all the stock and commodities exchanges now trade some form of stock index option. New ones are being created as fast as Federal regulators will permit. But the listings all follow the same form.

(TABLE 12) S & P 100 Index*				
1	**2**	**3**	**4**	**5**
STRIKE	**VOL**	**LAST**	**NET CHG**	**OPEN INT.**
Jan 720p	27	109	24⅛	61
Feb 630c	15	100	- 10⅞	314
Mar 750c	804	16½	+16	2754
Jan 765c	1424	1	+ ½	5552
Apr 780p	1	59½	—	1
Feb 800c	10	⅜	—	34

Call Vol 71,064   Open Int. 186,419
Put Vol 71,355   Open In. 261,781

*Transaction information for illustration only.

Column 1. The expiration date (3rd Friday of the month), the strike price and either a letter c for "call" or a letter p for "put." A buyer of a Feb 630c is betting that the Standard and Poor 500 Index (an index of the 500 stocks that are very heavily traded) will exceed 630 by the third Friday of February. That's not a bad bet, since on this day the index closed at 729.99 (a fact not shown on the table). By the same token, a buyer of the Apr 780p is betting that the index will be below 780 on the third Friday of April.

Column 2. Volume: 1,424 Jan 765 call options were traded. Trading stock index options is among the hottest games on Wall Street because it is such a convenient way to take (or hedge) a position on whether stocks in general will go up or down.

Column 3. The price at which the last option of the day traded. The Feb 630c (February calls at 630) closed at 100. Since the actual cash value of an index option is 100 times the listed price, someone—probably many people—paid $10,000 (100 times 100) for the Feb 630c.

Column 4. The change in price since the previous day's close. The Feb 630c's fell 10⅞. In other words, someone who owned one contract lost $1,088.75 (100 times 10⅞). This market attracts gamblers because price volatility can be so high. Note that the March 750 calls went from ½ to 16½ in a single day.

Column 5. The number of contracts outstanding. Unlike stocks, which represent the ownership in something tangible, the number of contracts—really bets—in existence can go up or down at the whim of investors. Stock index markets have become amazingly active, with tens or even hundreds of thousands of contracts around at one time. Believers see this as an achievement, facilitating complex investment and hedging strategies. Skeptics see it as confirmation that the securities markets are being transformed into casinos. The last time that happened, they argue, was the 1920s.

Commodity Futures

A commodity future contract is an agreement between a buyer and seller to trade a specific amount of a commodity at a date in the future: "I agree to sell you *A* tons of commodity *B* at $*C* a ton for delivery in *D* months." Got it? Go to the head of the class, or read on.

Organized futures markets for everything from coffee to lumber to platinum have been around for a long time. That's because businesses producing these commodities, along with businesses that use them as raw materials, need futures markets to hedge against the risk of price changes. For example, a jewelry manufacturer that must set catalogue prices a half-year in advance might lock in the cost of the gold she uses by purchasing gold in the futures market for delivery in six months. A farmer worried in the spring that corn prices might collapse by harvest time might sell corn for delivery in October.

What works to reduce risk for some also serves to in-

crease risk for others. In fact, many if not most of the buyers and sellers in the futures markets are speculators hoping to profit by correctly predicting changes in commodity prices. For heavily traded commodities, such as corn, wheat, soybeans, and vegetable oils, the average contract is held for only three to five days before it is sold for a gain or loss.

Some speculators are big winners, using the incredible leverage offered by futures contracts to double their investment in weeks. *But take care: by one estimate, five commodity speculators out of six lose money.* And far too many commodities brokers are hustlers who don't care whether you end up as one of the five.

By law, commodity futures may only be bought and sold through organized, government-regulated exchanges. The exchange is a go-between, linking likeminded buyers and sellers. But once a contract to deliver this much frozen orange juice concentrate at that many cents per pound is made, the exchange takes the responsibility to enforce the agreement. Technically, commodity futures agreements are with the exchange, not the other party. So there is never any worry that it will be necessary to take the other party to court.

Future contracts in corn are traded on the Chicago Board of Trade (CBT) exchange. Some fifteen different exchanges offer commodities futures, with virtually no overlap in commodities.

Immediately following the exchange symbol is the size of the standard contract and the units in which prices are

(TABLE 13)

COMMODITY FUTURES*

CORN (CBT) 5,000 BU.; CENTS PER BU.

1	2	3		4	5	6		7
						LIFETIME		OPEN
	OPEN	HIGH	LOW	SETTLE	CHANGE	HIGH	LOW	INTEREST
May	284½	284¾	282½	283¼	–¾	330	269¾	14,180
July	279¼	279¾	278¾	278¾	—	331	273	51,331
Sept	268¾	269½	268	268¾	+¼	321½	266½	12,100
Dec	263½	264½	262¾	263½	+½	295	260¾	5,167
Mar 94	271	272½	271	271¼	+¾	297	269¼	3,830
May 94	276	276¾	275½	276¼	+¾	291¼	274½	1,732
July 94	278	278¼	277¾	278	+¾	286	276¼	273

Est. vol. 20,000; vol. prev. day 16,602; open int. 108, 613, -1,408

*Transaction information for illustration only.

set. Thus corn (and most grains) come in standard units of 5,000 bushels, and prices are quoted in cents per bushel.

Column 1. The month in which the seller agrees to deliver the commodity. Commodity contracts are written for regular intervals specified by the exchange, with the longest contracts stretching about a year into the future.

Investors are betting on price changes. Sellers typically have no wish to deliver the commodity in question, nor do buyers really want to accept delivery. Thus most contracts are liquidated long before the delivery month by a transaction that balances out the original commitment. For example, the seller of eight December contracts for corn (40,000 bushels' worth) would simply buy eight December contracts when she wished to stop betting the price of corn would fall.

Past a certain "notice date"—in the case of corn, the last day of the month preceding the delivery month— sellers have the option of meeting their contractual obligation by delivering the commodity. When that happens, some unfortunate buyer designated under the rules of the exchange—usually the person who has held a buying contract longest—has no choice but to accept delivery. The moral: Buyers of corn (or other commodity) futures who don't want to risk finding a trainload of food on the doorstep some fine morning should be sure to liquidate their positions before the notice date.

Column 2. The price at which the first contract of the

day was struck. September corn sold for $2.6875 (268¾) per bushel. Corn for delivery in May 1994 went for $2.76.

These prices are really guesses about the future price of corn. Investors on the "buy" side of the contract hope that prices will rise because they have locked in the maximum they will have to pay. Investors on the "sell" side hope prices will fall.

Note one factor, though, that governs the relationship between prices for different monthly contracts. A futures price can never be higher than the price of buying the commodity today, plus lost interest on the investment in the commodity, plus storage and delivery costs. Otherwise, savvy traders could guarantee themselves an automatic profit by purchasing the commodity for cash and selling a futures contract for a like amount.

Column 3. The high and low contract prices for the day. The high for December corn was $2.645 a bushel; the low was $2.6275.

The exchanges impose limits on both the amount a futures price can vary from the closing price on the previous day (in the case of corn, 10 cents a bushel), and the range between the high and low on any single day (for corn, 20 cents a bushel). The idea is to prevent panic trading on news of an important event—for example, freezing weather for the citrus crop. When a limit is reached, the exchange doesn't close. It simply stops trading until a buyer and seller can be found who want to make a deal within the limit range.

Column 4. The price at which the last contract of the day was written. May 1993 corn futures closed at $2,8325; July 1994 closed at $2.78.

Buyers of futures contracts profit when futures prices rise. Suppose, for example, the price of the May 1993 contract rises by 20 cents to $3.0325. A buyer may cash in by selling a May 1993 contract, liquidating his position and realizing a profit of 20 cents a bushel, or $1,000.

The same arithmetic works in reverse for sellers. A seller would be free to close out his position by purchasing a May 1993 contract at a loss of 20 cents a bushel, or $1,000. Both buyers and sellers pay commissions to brokers for each trade. So the buyer who closed out his position would profit by a bit less than $1,000 and the seller would lose a bit more than $1,000.

Column 5. The change in the closing price since the previous trading day. The prices of corn futures fluctuate in units of a quarter of a penny a bushel. This minimum fluctuation (or "tick," in the jargon of the exchanges) varies from commodity to commodity.

The buyer of a May 1993 contract that day was committed to purchase 5,000 bushels of corn for $14,162.50 (5,000 times $2.8325.) Everyone knows the buyer is very unlikely to hold the contract to delivery. But the exchange does want to make certain that the buyer can, if necessary, make good on his commitment. Thus it requires both buyers and sellers to put up 5 to 10 percent of the value of the commodity as margin when the contract is made, much the way a building contractor is sometimes required to put up cash as a performance bond before beginning a project.

At the close of each trading day, the exchange "marks all positions to market." Suppose, for example, the price of May 1993 futures rises 5 cents. At the end of the day, the exchange will credit the margin accounts of everyone on the buy side of the contracts with a nickel a bushel, or $250 in cash per contract. And simultaneously, it will take $250 in cash from the margin accounts of all May 1993 sellers.

Those who receive cash are free to withdraw it from their accounts. When a buyer's or seller's margin is depleted to specified levels, the exchange can demand an infusion of cash. If the investor is unable to meet this call for margin money, his position is automatically liquidated.

Column 6. The range of contract prices since contracts with this delivery date were first created. For July 1993 corn futures, the range was from a high of $3.31 a bushel to a low of $2.73.

Consider how much money might have been made or lost by investors since the contract was created the previous year. Say a seller put down 10 percent as margin just when the contract peaked at $3.31 a bushel. That amounted to an investment of about 33 cents a bushel. By the time the July contract had bottomed out at $2.73, our lucky investor's margin account would have been credited with a profit of 58 cents a bushel (331 minus 273), or almost double his money.

By the same token, of course, a buyer of a July contract at 3.31 would have lost 58 cents a bushel. If he had not been willing or able to replenish his margin account with cash, he would long ago have been closed out.

Column 7. The number of contracts outstanding at the close of the trading day. Note that the open interest in July 1993 contracts is three times as large as the number of May 1993 contracts. That's because investors have been closing out their May positions as the possibility of delivery approaches. Note, too, how few contracts have been written for delivery dates in 1994. That's because businesses that use the futures markets for hedging and hold much of the open interest rarely plan so far ahead.

Some 20,000 contracts (for 100 million bushels of corn) were written that day, reflecting the immense liquidity of the markets for grain futures. By contrast, the futures markets for unleaded gasoline had a volume of only 262 contracts. Overall, open interest in corn fell by 1,408 contracts.

Financial Futures

Financial futures are contracts to deliver a financial instrument at a specified time for a specified price. The markets for financial futures work much like the markets for futures in commodities. Only instead of creating contracts for the future delivery of cotton or gold or heating oil, the contracts cover the delivery of U.S. Treasury bonds or German marks or U.S. Treasury bills. So most of the information provided in the key to the commodity futures table also applies to financial futures.

Treasury bond futures are traded on the Chicago Board of Trade (CBT) and the MidAmerica Commodity Exchange (MCE). The standard contract is for $100,000 on the CBT and $50,000 on the MCE. Unlike commodity contracts, some variation in what actually has to be delivered is permitted. For example, under exchange rules, Treasury bonds can be any issue of U.S. Treasury bonds with a remaining term of fifteen or more years. Thus a seller could deliver any of twenty issues with different maturity dates. Before trading in financial futures, be sure to find out what the rules of the exchange are.

Prices are quoted in fractional 32nds of a percentage point of face value. That is not the case for financial futures on securities with shorter maturities. Financial futures in Treasury bills and insured bank deposits trade in 100ths of a percentage point of face value.

Column 1. The month in which delivery of the bonds is due. Less than 3 percent of financial futures contracts are actually settled by delivery. *As with commodity futures, most traders close out their positions by undertaking the opposite transaction.* For example, an investor who is obliged to sell a bond in December 1994 can end the obligation by contracting to buy a bond in December 1994.

Column 2. The price at which the first contract of the day was struck. June 1993 contracts opened at 72-05, which translates as 72 and 5/32nds of a percent (72.1563 percent) of the $100,000 face value. To put it another way, someone contracted to buy a Treasury bond with a $100,000 value at maturity for delivery in June 1993 at a price of $72,156.30.

Column 3. The highest price at which contracts were written. For example, the June 1993s peaked at 72-19, which is 72 and 19/32nds of a percent of face value, or $72,593.80.

(TABLE 14)
FINANCIAL FUTURES*

TREASURY BONDS (CBT) — $100,000; PTS. 32NDS OF 100 PERCENT.

1	2	3	4	5		6	7		8	9
								YIELD		OPEN
	OPEN	HIGH	LOW	SETTLE	CHG		SETTLE	CHG.		INTEREST
June	72-05	72-19	71-31	72-01	+2		11.632	-.010		146,197
Sept	71-03	71-18	70-29	70-31	+2		11.814	-.011		42,399
Dec	70-06	70-18	69-31	70-01	+2		11.978	-.011		11,116
Mr94	69-11	69-23	69-04	69-06	+2		12.129	-.011		8,488
June	68-21	68-29	68-13	68-14	+1		12.266	-.006		6,194
Sept	67-31	68-09	67-24	67-24	··		12.394	··		3,818
Dec	67-13	67-20	67-05	67-05	··		12.506	··		1,684
Mr95	66-20	66-20	66-19	66-19	-1		12.613	+.006		976
Sept	66-02	66-09	65-20	65-20	-2		12.802	+.012		1,374

Est vol 160,000; vol prev 71,064; open int. 223,423, +1.

*Transaction information for illustration only.

Column 4. The lowest price at which contracts were written. Again looking at the June 1993s, the figure is 71-31, or 71 and 31/32nds of a percent of face value, or $71,968.70. The difference between the high and low that day was 20/32nds of a percentage point. Under exchange rules, by the way, the limit on the trading range for a single day is 64/32nds.

Column 5. The last price at which contracts were written that trading day.

Column 6. The change in the closing price since the previous day, in 32nds of a percentage point. Our June 1993s were up 2, which is 2/32nds of a percentage point of $100,000, or $62.50. That is a very modest change in price. But remember, one of the attractions of the futures market is that investors need not put much down to play the game. In the case of Treasury bonds, just $1,500 is required as margin. So an increase in value of $62.50 represented an increase of over 4 percent in a single day, or an annualized rate of gain of 1,520 percent!

Column 7. Futures for Treasury bonds and other fixed-return securities are often referred to as interest rate futures, and for good reason. Bond prices change in response to changes in interest rates. If interest rates rise, bond prices fall. And, of course, if interest rates fall, bond prices rise. *So an investment in a Treasury bond future is really a bet about the course of interest rates between the day you write the contract and the delivery date.*

The yield column is the interest return that corresponds to the closing price for the bond future. For the June 1993s that yield was 11.632 percent. Put it another way: if an investor purchased a Treasury bond in June 1993 for 72-01 ($72,031.25) and held the bond fifteen years to maturity, the annualized return would be 11.632 percent.

Column 8. The change in yield since the close of trading the previous day. For the June bonds, an increase in bond value of 2/32nds of a percentage point is equivalent to a reduction in yield of .01 percent.

Column 9. Open interest is the number of standard contracts in existence. There are 146,197 contracts outstanding for the June 1993 bonds. Open interest for other delivery dates is considerably less, but a quick look at the numbers show that this has become an incredibly large market. At the $1,500 initial margin requirement for buyer and seller, the 146,197 figure represents a total cash investment of $438,591 million (3,000 times 146,197).

The estimated volume of trading in all Treasury bond contracts was 160,000. Put it another way: investors in this market traded commitments with a total value of $16 billion!

There is no end to the wheels within wheels that make Wall Street spin. You now know about futures and options. Some genius (where there is a will there is a way) has combined the two to create options on futures, known as futures options. The concept is analogous to options trading in securities. But what's traded here are options—the right to sell or buy at a fixed price within a fixed time limit—on futures contracts. Among the types of futures: commodities, Treasury bonds, foreign currencies, stock indexes.

Are you lost? Join the crowd. While there is substantial trading in these strange derivative contracts, it's almost entirely between pros. If you needed to buy this book to interpret the financial pages, this is not the market for you.

Foreign Exchange

Currencies are traded electronically through a global "over-the-counter" market linking large banks and government agencies. This market is enormous and growing. In part that's because a torrent of foreign currency is needed to finance the trillion dollars' worth of goods and services—everything from Japanese cars to Brazilian steel to British oil—that flow between countries each year. In part, it's because corporate money managers have become increasingly sophisticated in searching for the highest, safest yields on their working capital. Every day, tens of billions of dollars' worth of currencies are moved from bank to bank and country to country in response to changing market conditions.

Column 1. The country and name of the currency. Note that Ecuador (and many other less-developed countries) shows both an "official" and a "floating" exchange rate.

The first is a rate set by the Ecuadorian government for certain types of transactions within the country. For example, foreign tourists may be legally required to purchase sucres from banks at the official rate. The floating rate is the free market exchange rate that may or may not be legally sanctioned. For example, Ecuadorians investing their savings abroad may be allowed to buy dollars with sucres at the floating rate, but not the lower, official rate.

"SDR" stands for the Special Drawing Rights created by an international organization in Washington called the International Monetary Fund. SDRs aren't currency in the usual sense. There is no place where you can buy a hamburger or a newspaper with a handful of SDR coins. The SDR is really an index of currency value based on a basket of U.S., German, French, British, and Japanese currencies. The International Monetary Fund keeps certain accounts in SDRs. And sometimes business contracts are written so that payment can be made in any of the individual currencies in the basket at its current exchange value with SDRs.

"ECU" stands for European Currency Unit. Like the SDR, it is more an index than a currency. The value of an ECU is the weighted average of the value of a bunch of European currencies. ECUs are largely used as a unit of exchange within Europe. Sometimes private contracts are written with prices in ECUs but payable in any major world currency.

Column 2. The number of U.S. dollars it would take to buy a unit of currency that day at 4:00 P.M. New York time. Stock market transactions are usually quoted for the end of the trading day. But dollars are being bought and sold around the clock somewhere in the world. Hence the logic of quoting exchange rates at a time when trading is open in America, but closed in the major currency markets in Europe and Asia.

According to the table, it cost $1.22 to purchase a British pound. That is the price at which banks traded pounds in million-dollar lots. An individual buying a few thousand dollars' worth would have to pay between 2 and 10 percent more.

Note the 30-, 90-, and 180-day "forward" rates quoted for British pounds. A forward rate is the rate at which a currency can be purchased for delivery on some specified date in the future. Forward currency markets exist between the half-dozen currencies used for world trade, and for good reason.

Forward currency contracts are useful for people who have a bill to pay in a foreign currency weeks or months in the future and don't want to take the risk that exchange rates will change in the meantime. Consider an American importer who agrees to pay 16 pounds each for wool sweaters from Britain when they arrive in Houston in 90 days. To lock in the exact number of dollars the sweaters will cost, she buys 90-day forward pounds at a rate of $1.1988 per pound (plus brokerage commissions).

Column 3. The number of dollars it took to buy a unit of foreign currency twenty-four hours earlier. Note that

British currency was almost 4 percent cheaper for Americans on Monday than on Tuesday. By historical standards, that is a dramatically rapid shift in rates. But in recent years rapid shifts have become quite common, reflecting both an explosion of speculation in foreign currencies and the unwillingness of governments to intervene in the currency markets to dampen the shifts in currency values.

Column 4. The number of units of foreign currency it would take to buy a dollar. The information in this column complements the information in column two. But in some cases, it is easier to use. Thus, while it may take a pocket calculator to figure out what a dollar-cruzeiro exchange value of .0002024 means, the idea of 4940 cruzeiros to the dollar is a snap to comprehend.

Column 5. Exchange rates twenty-four hours earlier, complementing the information in column 3.

(TABLE 15)
FOREIGN EXCHANGE*

1	2	3	4	5
	U.S. $ EQUIVALENT		CURRENCY PER U.S. $	
COUNTRY	TUES.	MON.	TUES.	MON.
Brazil (Cruzeiro)	.0002024	.0002024	4940.00	4940.00
Britain (Pound)	1.2200	1.1820	.8200	.8291
30-Day Forward	1.2155	1.1773	.8827	.8324
90-Day Forward	1.2079	1.1698	.8279	.8378
180-Day Forward	1.1988	1.1602	.8342	.8447
Ecuador (Sucre)				
Official rate	.01489	.01489	67.18	67.18
Floating rate	.008849	.008849	113.00	113.00
SDR	0.979662	0.976173	1.02076	1.02441
ECU	0.702132	0.690176	..	..

*Transaction information for illustration only.

99

PART TWO

The Numbers

Stock Market Indexes

Are stocks up or down? By how much? It's easy to answer the question for any individual stock: if IBM sold for 130 yesterday and 132 today, it must have gone up two dollars a share, or about 1.54 percent. But stock prices change by varying percentages and in different directions. The search for a single number to describe what's happening to the whole market led to the creation of the stock indexes.

The indexes are averages of stock prices, in some cases adjusted for the relative size of the companies included and set at some nice round number for a base year value. The adjustment, or "weighting," is meant to assure that a 1-percent increase in the stock of a company with a market value of $1 billion counts just one-twentieth as much as a 1-percent increase in a $20 billion company. The base year adjustment—say, setting 1990 equal to 100—makes for easy comparisons over time. If, for example, our hypothetical index reached 200 in 2000, it would be obvious that stock prices had doubled over the decade.

Dow Jones Industrial Average. The most frequently quoted index—the one they always flash on the evening news shows—is the Dow Jones Industrial Average. *For all its fame, though, "the Dow" isn't a very useful index.* In part that's because it includes only thirty companies. They may have been representative of industrial America in 1945, but no more. The thirty (beginning with AT&T, ending with Woolworth) are mostly "smokestack" companies. For example, three chemical companies (Du Pont, 3M, Union Carbide) are included, but only one computer company (IBM).

The Dow can also be misleading because it is not weighted by the relative size of the companies comprising the index. Thus a two point rise in J.P. Morgan or Woolworth stock has the same effect on the index as a two point rise in General Motors or IBM.

Perhaps the reason the Dow is so popular is because it has been around so long. Charles Dow, the publisher of the *Wall Street Journal,* started keeping daily records of the index in 1884. More likely, though, it's because people like big numbers. Somehow it just seems more exciting to speculate about whether the Dow will break 7,000 this year than, say, to ponder the probability that the average price of a share will rise 16 percent by December.

Dow Jones Utility Average. The Utility Average covers

fifteen big natural gas and electricity utilities. Since the prices of utility stocks used to fluctuate more or less consistently with interest rates, the average was often read as a barometer of what investors thought would happen to rates in the near future. But in recent years factors such as the demand for electric power, the attitudes of regulators, and public hostility to nuclear power have influenced utility prices, too.

Dow Jones Transportation Average. The Transportation Average tracks the fortunes of twenty transport companies. All twenty used to be railroads, but in recent years six airlines and three trucking companies have been substituted for a like number of choo-choo stocks. The most careful followers of the Transportation Index are believers in the Dow Theory. Dow theorists claim that stock prices go up or down in long waves. The tricky part, apparently, is distinguishing short-term movements from the long-term trend.

One clue, the Dowists claim, is whether both the Transportation and the Industrial averages are leading in the same direction. If, for example, the DJIA spurts up but the Transportation Average lingers behind, chances are the market upswing is temporary. However, if both averages enjoy solid gains, it's time to buy.

The trouble with the Dow Theory (and many similar "technical" theories) is that the theorists are a little vague about how much the averages have to change to mark a clear signal of a major market move. *Statistical analysis is sticky stuff. Beware stock market prophets bearing newsletters.*

The Standard and Poor's 500 Index. The S&P 500 has all the virtues and none of the vices of the Dow. It includes many more common stocks (400 industrial, 40 financial, 20 transportation, and 40 utility companies). It is weighted by the total value of shares outstanding, so fluctuations in the stock price of big companies count proportionately more than fluctuations in little ones. And because statisticians have gone to the trouble of grafting it to a much older capitalization-based index, the S&P 500 can be used to compare market averages all the way back to 1893. The Industrial, Financial, Transportation, and Utility components of the S&P 500 are also published separately.

Experts use the S&P 500 as a benchmark of overall market performance. If, for example, your mutual fund did no better over the last decade than this broadbased index, it's pretty clear the fund's managers have not earned their keep.

By the way, several mutual funds, most notably, the Vanguard Index Trust, do not even try to beat the average, but simply to match it. As money is added to the fund, it buys stocks in proportion to their weighting on the S&P 500. *So-called index funds (there are many others available to pension systems, bank trust departments, and other institutional investors) are very popular with business-school types who don't believe that anyone can expect to beat the market for very long.*

The New York Stock Exchange Composite Index. Another broad-based index, this one a value-weighted index of all the companies listed on the New York Stock Exchange. Typically, it tracks the changes in the S&P 500 because the 500 companies in the latter represent a large part of the value of the NYSE Index. Remember, though, only large companies are permitted to join the New York Stock Exchange. So in times when the stocks of smaller companies are particularly hot (or particularly cold), the NYSE may diverge from other indexes.

That, by the way, is where two other value-weighted indexes, the *American Stock Exchange Market Value Index* and the *NASDAQ Over-the-Counter Composite Index,* fit in. The former covers all the stocks on the American Stock Exchange. Since they are, on average, much smaller than the companies on the New York Stock Exchange, this index is a better indicator of what investors think about medium-large (smallish-large?) businesses. The NASDAQ index of about 3,500 stocks includes still smaller companies. It tends to be more volatile than the New York or American indexes because many of the companies traded over the counter are "go-go" stocks that operate on a roller coaster of investor optimism and pessimism.

The Wilshire 5000 Index. Looking for the very best index? There is no single best because each measures different things which are important to different people.

*However, if "best" means broadest based, the easy win-
ner is the Wilshire 5000.* It covers over 5,000 stocks,
weighted by capitalization. Most newspapers don't pub-
lish it on a daily basis, but you can find it in the *Wall
Street Journal* and the *New York Times.*

Interest Rates

Federal Funds Rate. Reported daily in major newspapers, usually as a high, low, and closing rate. This is the interest banks charge each other for one-day loans of $1 million or more. Banks are required to hold a minimum percentage of their assets as currency in the vault, or as no-interest deposits with the Federal Reserve. So at the end of each business day, banks that don't have enough reserves on hand to satisfy the Government borrow from those that have an excess. The transfers, totalling tens of billions of dollars each day, are all managed by computer.

Well, you probably aren't in the banking business, and you don't want to borrow $1 million. Why should you care what Citibank charges the Bank of America? *Because the federal funds rate is the single best measure of the current cost of money.*

The federal funds rate is a "pure" interest rate, one without any premium for the risk of default. A lender incurs no risk since the transaction amounts to an electronic transfer credit between accounts at a government agency. Nothing, moreover, inhibits the federal funds rate from fluctuating rapidly. Thus changes in the rate are a good indicator of what the Federal Government and other big debtors—and ultimately, you—will have to pay for credit in the coming days and weeks. By the same token, it offers hints about what will happen to the price of bonds and interest-sensitive stocks, such as electric utilities.

Broker Call Loan Rate. Reported daily in major newspapers, this is the rate (or range of rates) stockbrokers charge for loans secured by stocks and bonds in your brokerage account. It tracks changes in the federal funds rate pretty closely because it represents a convenient alternative for banks that would otherwise loan excess reserves to other banks.

The rate is a bit higher than the federal funds rate, typically a percentage point higher. But it is still the very cheapest source of credit for individuals. *If you own stocks, use this borrowing privilege before considering a personal loan from a bank or credit card.*

Prime Rate. Reported daily. It is the rate banks say they charge on loans to their very best corporate customers. Often it is also used as a base for calculating rates on other loans. A bank might, for example, set the rate it charges to smaller, less creditworthy businesses as the prime rate plus two percentage points.

In theory, different banks could set their prime rates at different levels and change them as frequently as they like. In practice, big banks in big cities usually match the rates charged by leading lenders, such as Morgan Guaranty, Bank of America, and Chase. And unlike the federal funds rate, banks rarely adjust their prime more than every month or two. A change can thus be big news, signaling a tightening or loosening of credit in the economy.

A decade ago, the prime was just what banks claimed it was. But today, many banks tell white lies, lending to customers they really want to attract at rates below the prime. The prime has become a bit like the official coach fare posted by airlines. That's the fare airlines charge customers who are least sensitive to cost and least able to shop around. Then it fills the empty seats by charging lower rates to people who would otherwise fly some other airline, or not fly at all.

Foreign Prime Rates. Reported daily in the *Wall Street Journal.* Though not strictly comparable to the American prime rates, the rates printed for Canada, Britain, Germany, Switzerland, and Japan do give a good indication of what it costs big, creditworthy customers to borrow in foreign currencies.

Those rates are sometimes higher, sometimes lower than the American prime. That's because lenders and borrowers who are as at home in one currency as another must factor in a guess about relative movements in exchange rates.

Suppose a Japanese oil refiner needs funds to import crude oil from the Middle East. The refiner could borrow Japanese yen at Japanese interest rates then convert the yen to dollars to pay off the sheiks. Or the refiner could borrow dollars in New York at higher, American interest rates.

Why would the refiner ever borrow the more expensive dollars? Because the refiner may figure that the dollar will depreciate in value sufficiently to compensate for the higher interest rate. If, for example, interest rates were four percentage points higher in dollars, but the dollar depreciated by five percent (relative to yen) over the course of a year when the loan was to be repaid, the Japanese refiner would be better off borrowing in dollars. So national differences in the prime rates are really the market's guess about what will happen to currency exchange rates.

Treasury Bill Rates. Auction results reported weekly; secondary market reported daily in most newspapers. Treasury bills—U.S. government bonds that mature in less than one year—are auctioned every Monday by the Federal Reserve. Once rates are determined competitively, smaller investors are permitted to buy bills at the average rate.

T-bills are sold in $10,000 minimums in "discount" form. The buyer initially pays less than the face value of the bond. The difference, around $250 on a $10,000 bill that matures in 90 days, represents the interest. There is a flourishing "secondary" market for T-bills, with billions' worth traded in each day. So it is always possible to tailor a purchase to a precise number of weeks, or own a bill in a single day. Banks and brokers handle the transactions for fairly modest fees. See page 44 for the details on how to read the numbers for this secondary market.

The T-bill rate is perhaps the most important rate for individual investors to follow. Next to the federal fund rate, it is probably the most sensitive indicator of interest rate trends in the economy. *Most important, it is the yardstick by which money market funds and banks compete for investors' cash.* Thus an increase in the T-bill rate this week will almost certainly translate into a rise in the rates paid by the banks and funds.

The Other Numbers

How're we doing? It may be easy to add up your personal scorecard—earnings, job promotions, and the like. But measuring the performance of the economy and predicting its future is another matter entirely. Here are some of the numbers the experts use in lieu of a crystal ball. You'll generally find them in news stories rather than statistical columns.

Output

Gross National Product (GNP). The total value of the finished goods and services produced in the economy. Note the word "finished." *In order to avoid counting output more than once, the GNP doesn't include the value of, say, the wheat that goes into making Wheaties.* But it does, of course, include the wheat that is sold abroad as raw wheat.

GNP is not a precise measure of national economic well-being. But "real" GNP (the GNP adjusted for inflation) may be the closest single number we've got to such a measure. The rate of growth of the GNP is reported every three months by the Commerce Department. Note that GNP growth (and most other rates reported by the government) is "annualized." If, for example, the GNP rose by 1.1 percent in the quarter of a year between March 31 and June 30, the annualized growth rate would be four times 1.1 percent, or 4.4 percent.

When the economy is coming out of a recession, GNP can grow quite quickly, sometimes at an annualized rate as high as 8 or 9 percent. That's because there is plenty of unused economic capacity, and managing rapid growth is only a matter of getting people and machines back to work.

But over the long run, the size of the work force, the quantity of capital, and the rate of productivity change put a ceiling on the growth rate of GNP. Very young economies that are just putting modern production techniques into place—for example, Japan early in this century—have sometimes grown at 10 percent annually for decades. *But mature economies like ours probably couldn't manage more than 3 percent a year for very long.* That is why very rapid growth of GNP creates the fear that inflation is on the way.

Industrial Production. A measure of industrial output is published once a month by the Federal Reserve. Unlike the gross national product, this number is an index in which production is measured by a benchmark of 100 set in 1990. If, for example, the industrial output index were 127 this month, it would mean the rate of output was 27 percent greater than in 1990.

Industrial production includes mining, manufacturing, and energy, but it omits one whopping big chunk of GNP: transportation, services, and agriculture. It is more volatile than GNP: in a modern recession in which GNP slips by 2 or 3 percent, it isn't unusual for industrial production to fall by 10 percent.

Productivity

Capacity Utilization. This number, published monthly by the Federal Reserve, is an estimate of the percentage of factory capacity that is being used. The highest it can possibly be is 100. But capacity utilization rarely exceeds 90 percent, and for good reason. All manufacturing facilities have a rate of output at which production costs are lowest. Above the rate, costs typically go up quickly because workers must be paid overtime, because machines wear out at accelerated speeds, and because there isn't adequate opportunity for the maintenance of equipment.

It may pay a company to exceed this efficient rate of capacity utilization for brief periods in order to fill orders. During World War II, many factories exceeded their efficient production rate for years. *But very high rates of utilization for the economy as a whole—over 85 percent—suggest that inflation is on the way.*

Labor Productivity. Reported quarterly by the Department of Labor, this number is an estimate of the output of the economy divided by the number of work hours it took to produce it.

Interpreting this number is tricky. Compared over decades, labor productivity is a crucial measure of economic success or failure. *If productivity grows rapidly, the chances are excellent that the benefits will be broadly enjoyed in the form of higher wages and higher living standards.* If productivity doesn't grow, the only way the average worker can live better is if (a) he or she puts in longer hours, or (b) a larger percentage of total output is paid in wages rather than interest or profit.

But as the economy cycles from prosperity to recession and back, other factors are at work that make it difficult to interpret productivity changes in the short run. Labor productivity virtually always goes up during recessions because the least efficient workers—and machines—are generally laid off first. For similar reasons, productivity usually falls as business scrambles to put labor and capital back to work.

Many economists would argue, though, that some of the productivity growth during recessions is the healthy result of greater competition for business survival. Under the pressure of falling profits and the threat of lost jobs, labor and management are forced to do their jobs better. This is the closest thing to a plausible rationale for why lean times may lead to fat.

Employment

*U*nemployment rate. Reported monthly by the Labor Department, this is an estimate of the percentage of people who are unemployed and are actively looking for work. Month-to-month changes of one- or two-tenths of a percentage point, even after adjustments for the seasonal ebb and flow of the supply and demand for labor, don't tell much. A big strike, or simply errors in estimation, may be the cause. So, too, may fluctuations in the number of "discouraged" workers—chronically unemployed workers who give up looking and thus cease to be part of the official statistics. *But larger changes over periods of several months tell a lot about how well the economy is doing and how hard it is to find work.*

The unemployment figures are broken down into groups by race, sex, and age. Unemployment of adult males usually tracks overall economic activity best.

Female unemployment is always higher than male, unemployment of blacks is higher yet, unemployment of black teenagers highest of all (it is not unusual for 40 percent of the last group to be looking in vain for work). In part this is due to racial and sexual discrimination in hiring. But there are other causes, too. Many employers believe that younger workers and female workers are less likely to stay on the job. And there is no question that a higher percentage of young, black, and female workers lack skills and experience.

During recessions, overall unemployment may run as high as 10 or 11 percent. Even in the best of times, millions of people are unemployed. This persistent level of joblessness has led economists to theorize about the "natural" rate of unemployment. When unemployment falls below this rate, employers have trouble matching qualified job seekers to the available work. To get the workers they want, they raise the wages offered. The higher labor costs are then passed on to consumers in the form of higher prices. Higher prices, in turn, lead to demands for still higher wages. The resulting wage-price spiral is only broken when unemployment again rises above the natural rate.

All that may sound reasonable. But why should the unemployment rate at which prices are stable be as high as 4 or 5 percent of the work force?

Conservatives focus on the role of economic incentives: Unemployment compensation, welfare, and high income tax rates make workers choosier about the jobs they are willing to take. Unions, minimum wages, and high social security wage taxes make employers less willing or able to hire workers without experience or proven skills. Liberals emphasize social factors: discrimination, rapid shifts in the location of industry, poor schools, and inadequate training programs.

Employment-Population Ratio. Reported monthly by the Labor Department, this is the percentage of the population over age sixteen that is employed. *Quarter-to-quarter changes in this number offer more insight into the "tightness" of the labor market than the unemployment figures because it includes everyone, not just people actively looking for work.* Over longer periods, though, the meaning of trends in the employment-population ratio is muddied by very complicated factors. For example, the reentry of married women into the labor force in the 1970s substantially raised the ratio. And in the future it may be altered by changing attitudes toward retirement.

Average Work Weeks and Average factory overtime. Reported monthly by the Department of Labor. Given the choice, most managers would rather adjust the number of hours workers put in than hire new employees or fire old ones. It's true that overtime is costly: the law requires time-and-a-half pay. But changing the work force is even costlier. New workers must be trained. Firing workers raises the taxes employers must pay into state unemployment compensation funds. And since most managers do have the choice, the average work week and average overtime hours both respond more quickly to the changing demand for labor than do employment figures.

The Money Supply

Each Thursday afternoon after the stock exchanges have closed, an independent government agency called the Federal Reserve releases a long list of financial statistics. They are published the next morning, in some cases in abbreviated form, in most big city newspapers. To the uneducated reader, the weekly Fed statistics are about as interesting (and about as comprehensible) as the Jakarta telephone directory. And twenty years ago hardly anybody except a few professionals bothered to decipher them.

Most economists, including many who believe that long-term trends in the supply of money are useful in predicting interest rates, economic growth, inflation, and stock prices, argue that these weekly statistics don't mean very much. The numbers are too heavily influenced, they say, by extraneous factors.

Nonetheless, Fed watching has become a passion on

Wall Street. *If enough people believe the weekly numbers mean the same thing and act on their interpretations, their views can be self-fulfilling.* Here, very briefly, is what they may be thinking.

Money is the grease which allows the wheels of the "real" economy—the factories, shops, farms, etc.—to turn. If there is too little of it, the price of borrowing money goes up. Higher interest rates mean lower prices for bonds and other securities which pay a fixed-dollar return. They also mean less demand for items bought on credit, everything from machine tools to autos to houses. And that means higher costs and less profit for businesses that sell to credit-sensitive customers. *So "tight" money can also lend to lower stock prices.*

Too much money, on the other hand, generates a different set of risks for investors. When banks have more money to lead, interest rates tend to fall. Accordingly, bond and stock prices tend to rise. But that is only the initial effect. Too much money chasing too few goods creates inflation. If the prices of goods and services go up, or if lenders and borrowers expect prices to go up in the near future, interest rates will also go up.

It's easy to see why. If lenders believe they will be paid back in dollars with less purchasing power, they will insist on more interest as compensation. If borrowers believe the same thing, they will be more willing to pay the higher rates. So inflation, or the expectation of inflation, can lead to higher interest rates. And this, in turn, leads to both lower bond and stock prices.

That leaves not one, but two, $64 questions: How do

you measure the quantity of money? How much money is not too little and not too much, but jus-s-s-st right?

Everybody knows what money is—the silver and green stuff in your pocket. Along with cash, though, you would certainly want to include the money in your checking account. Now things get trickier. How about bank savings deposits? Shares in money market funds? U.S. Savings Bonds? U.S. Treasury securities that can be turned into cold cash with a phone call to your broker?

The experts don't agree, so the Fed keeps track of several different series of money supply numbers, three of which are published weekly:

M1. The most conservative definition of money. It consists of currency and bank checking deposits held by the public, plus credit union deposits and travelers' checks issued by companies that aren't banks.

M2. A much broader definition to include more assets that can be quickly converted to spendable form. It consists of everything in M1, plus money market fund shares owned by individuals, plus uninsured overnight loans to banks, plus savings accounts, plus bank savings certificates in sums smaller than $100,000. Deposits in retirement accounts are excluded.

M3. A still broader definition. Everything in M2 plus bank savings certificates larger than $100,000, plus uninsured loans to banks that are backed by U.S. Treasury securities, plus dollar deposits in overseas branches of American banks, plus money market fund shares owned by pension funds and other institutions.

A fourth, less-often used definition of money that goes beyond M3 is called L. It consists of M3 plus all other easily measured liquid assets in the economy that could serve the function of money: U.S. Treasury bills, U.S. Savings Bonds, short-term debts of blue-chip corporations (called commercial paper), tradable short-term debts from corporations to banks (called bankers' acceptances), dollar deposits by U.S. residents in European banks (called Eurodollars).

Like all definitions of money, of course, L doesn't quite describe what we want to know because it can't measure the intentions of the people who own the assets.

Now for that second question. *Twenty years ago, most economists would have said the right amount of money was simply the amount that kept interest rates stable. Today, most are fence sitters:* they still believe that money drives the economy through its effect on interest rates. But they accept the idea that the changes in the quantity of money create expectations of inflation and therefore have an independent effect on economic growth and securities prices.

So the Federal Reserve's Open Market Committee—the seven presidentially appointed members of the Federal Reserve Board plus three heads of regional Federal

Reserve banks—periodically set targets for growth of each of the money supply aggregates. The target rates are supposed to allow for the creation of enough money to permit the economy to grow without increasing inflationary pressures.

That, of course, only begs the original question. *There is no generally accepted theory of how much money is enough.* In the real world much seems to turn on the market's belief that the people in charge will do whatever is needed, including sacrificing economic growth and employment, to hold the line on prices. When the target rates for money supply growth are exceeded for several weeks in a row, or when the Chairman of the Federal Reserve suggests that inflation may not be so terrible after all, many investors get edgy. *And right or wrong, if they're edgy, maybe you should be, too.*

A last issue of some confusion: Once the Fed sets targets for the money supply numbers, how does it go about hitting them?

The Fed's primary method is "open market" operations. If it wants to increase the supply, it buys government bonds that are owned by the public. The public swaps bonds, which aren't part of the money supply, for Fed-issued cash and checks, which are. If the Fed want to reduce the money supply, it reverses the process, selling government bonds that it already owns. The public gives up checking deposits, which are part of the money supply, for bonds, which aren't.

It sounds simple; in practice it's pretty messy. Sometimes the Fed tries to increase the money supply, but the independent actions of private lenders and borrowers off-set their actions. For the same reasons, the Fed sometimes overshoots. Given enough time, such mistakes can be corrected. But Wall Street remains fixated by the weekly money supply numbers.

Inflation

The Consumer Price Index. Reported monthly by the Labor Department. The concept, if not the execution, is a snap. The government surveys the price of a market basket of goods which is supposed to represent the average consumer's buying habits. It includes everything from T-shirts to T-Birds in rough proportion to the amounts actually purchased. This dollar figure is then adjusted to an index number, based on a value of 100 for the period 1982 through 1984. If, for example, the index were 168.4 this month, the goods and services that cost an average of $100 in the years 1982 through 1984 cost $168.40 today.

For most purposes, changes in the index are of more interest than the level. They are usually reported as an annualized percentage. If, for example, the index went up by four-tenths of a percent last month, the annualized rate would be twelve times that fraction, of 4.8 percent.

Just to confuse matters, there are two CPIs. The one

most commonly cited, the CPI-W, tracks the prices paid by all wage earners and clerical workers. The other, the CPI-U, follows the prices paid by consumers in urban areas. But not to worry: since the two indexes don't diverge all that much, the distinction hardly matters to most of us. The people who may care, though, are workers and retirees whose monthly checks are linked to one index or the other.

Two points to think about. First, the CPI is an average of everybody's prices. *Since you aren't likely to buy the same goods in the same proportion as the average person, the CPI doesn't really reflect your cost of living.* If, for example, you buy a lot of books or drink a lot of wine or fly frequently on airplanes, you've done better than the CPI over the last decade because the prices of these goods and services have lagged behind inflation. On the other hand, if you eat out a lot or rent an apartment rather than own a house, you've done worse.

Second, the CPI is really an overestimate of how much the cost of living has changed for the average person. That's because the index can't take into account quality improvements in existing products or the introduction of new ones.

Don't believe it matters much? Try this experiment. Browse through one of those reproductions of an old turn-of-the-century Sears catalogue. Then ask yourself whether you would rather have $1,000 to spend on the old items at the old prices, or $1,000 to spend at Sears today at current prices. Some of the old products, like simple hand tools, would be a great bargain at the old prices. But the same can't be said for the washing machines or toasters. And the comparison doesn't even make sense for new inventions like stereos or video recorders.

The Producer Price Index. Reported monthly by the Labor Department. The PPI used to be called the Wholesale Price Index, which is what it really is: the price that producers of finished goods charge to their customers. Like other price indexes, it is an estimate of the changes in costs of a "basket" of goods. Like the CPI, it is adjusted to an index level, where prices in 1982 are arbitrarily set at 100.

The PPI is more sensitive to changes in the costs of raw materials and somewhat less sensitive to changes in the cost of labor than the Consumer Price Index. That's because the costs PPI leaves out—in particular, retailing and advertising—are almost entirely labor costs.

The PPI is particularly interesting because it's a pretty good forecaster of consumer prices to come. *If producer prices are stable, the prices of goods passed on to consumers over the coming months will probably be stable, too.* If not, watch out.

Unit Labor Costs. Reported quarterly by the Department of Labor. This is an index of total output by private firms in the economy, divided by total labor compensation—wages, fringes, and social security. The number is then fitted to an index, with 1987 equal to 100. If, for example, the index were 121.5 today, output that used $100 worth of labor to make in 1982 now uses $121.50 worth of labor to make.

Actually, trends in this index can be more useful than the level. Over long periods of time, there need not be a fixed relationship between prices in the economy and unit labor costs. Companies might, for example, shift to production processes that use much more or much less labor without greatly affecting the cost of the product. Over a period of a few years, though, the links between labor costs and product costs can be pretty close. *If unit labor costs are rising more rapidly than consumer prices, labor is apparently becoming scarce, and inflationary pressures are building in the economy.* If, on the other hand, unit labor costs are falling behind changes in the overall price level, inflationary pressures are cooling.

Economic Indicators

Corporate Profits. Estimated quarterly by the *Wall Street Journal* and (separately) by the Department of Commerce. The *Journal* surveys the profits of about 500 companies, publishing a report about a month after the quarter ends. The Commerce Department survey, published three weeks later, covers most of corporate America.

Profit, of course, is what's left over after other expenses—taxes, wages, rent, and materials—have been paid. And since business cannot rapidly adjust the size of its labor force or production capacity, profits bear the brunt of ups and downs in the economy. *Thus in a recession in which output falls by 2 percent, profits may drop by 20 percent or more.* What works on the way down also works on the way up: during booms, profits rise much more rapidly than output or total wages.

Profit is also the reward for ownership. The more companies earn, the more the stock is worth. So you might expect that stock prices would rise (or fall) with news from the quarterly surveys. In fact, the market's response is not so predictable.

Sophisticated investors know about cycles in profitability and take them into account when they decide to buy or sell. But unanticipated quarterly results—profits that are either higher or lower than generally expected—do affect stock prices. Grim news will almost certainly lower stock prices. Very good results will raise stock prices, provided investors do not interpret the news as a harbinger of general inflationary pressure in the economy.

Most economists used to believe that stocks were a good hedge against the value-eroding effects of inflation. As the general price level went up, they argued, the average corporation should be able to maintain its profitability by selling its products for more money. But markets don't run by theories. And, in fact, stocks took a terrible beating during the inflation of the 1970s. Ever since, people have been debating why.

One straightforward explanation is that investors believe that inflation always leads to recession. Thus they anticipate that profits will inevitably fall in real terms when the government responds to inflation by tightening fiscal and monetary policies.

A more complicated hypothesis, one now widely accepted by economists, is that the effective rate of taxation on profits goes up with inflation. In times of rapidly rising prices, the cost of replacing worn-out equipment also rises. But the tax laws treat these costs as an unvarying constant, and thus force companies to pay profits taxes on funds that should properly go to replace depreciated assets. So, the theory goes, more inflation leads to lower real after-tax profits, which in turn leads to a lower valuation for stocks.

Got it? Don't worry if you don't. *The important thing to remember is that the stock market is probably a bad place to invest if you expect inflation to heat up.*

Personal Disposable Income. Reported monthly by the Commerce Department. Take the sum of private earnings—wages, salaries, pensions, dividends, interest, and rent. Add government "transfer payments," such as unemployment insurance, social security benefits, welfare, and veterans' benefits. Then subtract taxes paid by individuals, including social security deductions. What's left is a measure of personal spending power, what individuals have to divide between consumption and savings.

PDI (and its change from previous months) is interesting for a bunch of reasons. *To begin, it is one good, bottom-line measure of how well or poorly we are doing as a group.* Other statistics, such as GNP, are at least one step removed from personal spending power. Personal income never falls as far or as fast as national output during a recession. That's because the federal government acts as a buffer, collecting less taxes and paying out more in benefits.

For stock market watchers, personal income is a good indicator of the ability of the public to buy autos, appliances, air travel, and other goods whose purchase can be postponed. *A flat or falling PDI is thus bad news for these highly cyclical industries.* Remember, though, rising personal income does not guarantee rising purchases. If people have badly depleted their savings during a recession or simply fear that another downturn is on the way, they may be reluctant to spend.

Inventories. Reported monthly by the Department of Commerce. Inventories are supplies, products in the process of being manufactured, and unfinished goods yet to be sold by businesses. The drums of paint waiting to cover Chevy Luminas at a General Motors plant represent inventory. So do the tape cassette decks ready to be installed in the Luminas, and the thousands of Luminas already in transit to dealers. So, too, for that matter, is the spare roll of paper towels in the executive washroom at the Lumina plant.

From a company's perspective, the choice of how much inventory to carry is often a critical and difficult decision. A lot of inventory reduces the possibility you'll run out of supplies or finished product in periods of unanticipated demand. But, by the same token, it costs money to carry inventory—money to carry the investment in supplies, money to maintain storage facilities, and money to insure their contents.

Japanese factories make a fetish of carrying a bare minimum of inventories. In some, supplies of critical assembly parts are designed to last just a few hours. Suppliers, located within a few miles, are expected to replenish parts several times a day. Nothing comparable is possible in the U.S. because supplies must be shipped great distances, often in unreliable weather. But there is little question that the Japanese example, plus a decade of very high interest rates, led many American companies to work harder at paring inventories.

For the economy-watcher, monthly inventory figures offer valuable clues about the direction of output. As the economy moves smartly out of recession, the growth in sales outpaces inventories; thus inventories measured as a percentage of monthly sales begin to shrink. So very low inventory figures suggest the economy is taking off, or at very least, ready to grow because sales are outpacing demand. By similar logic, growth in inventories relative to sales is a warning that the economy is poised for recession.

Orders for Nondefense Capital Goods. Reported monthly by the Commerce Department. Capital goods consist of industrial products used to make other products. Some level of spending on capital goods is needed simply to replace worn-out or obsolete machinery. Some is always needed to take advantage of new cost-cutting technology or for the manufacture of new products. But orders for capital goods are largely dependent on what business thinks sales will be in the future.

That makes outstanding orders for capital goods a useful barometer for the business cycle. Orders usually lag far behind recovery from a recession. For one thing, businesses doubt the recovery will last; for another, they usually begin an upswing with plenty of unused capacity.

But since there is often a long wait between an order for equipment and its delivery, companies must eventually commit themselves to purchases or risk losing business.

High and continuing demand for capital goods is thus a good indication from the people who know best that a recovery is strong. On the other hand, weak demand suggests that the recovery may be limited and short-lived.

Orders for Machine Tools. Reported monthly by the National Machine Tool Dealers Association. Machine tools are machines that shape parts. A few decades ago, most were interchangeable in many plants and processes—simple drill presses, lathes, plastic extruding machines, etc. Today, many are specialized hi-tech wonders that perform dozens of operations in sequence without human intervention.

Machine tools are a sub-category of capital goods. Thus it shouldn't be surprising that the two categories follow similar cyclical patterns. *What makes machine tools special is that the swings in demand are far more dramatic.* When companies that make capital goods are convinced that business is on the rise, machine tool orders may double in a matter of months. Collapses in sales can be just as dramatic.

Index of Leading Indicators. Reported monthly by the Commerce Department. All sorts of statistics provide hints about what will happen to the level of economic activity over the next few months. But none is consistently accurate, and business economists fiercely dispute the pros and cons of each. What to do?

The Commerce Department's answer is the practical equivalent of delegating responsibility to a committee. Instead of picking one statistic, they offer an index constructed from twelve different statistics. Components of the index are:

- The money supply (the Federal Reserve's broad M2 definition)
- Outstanding loans to business and consumers
- An index of raw materials prices
- Stock market prices (the Standard and Poor 500 index)
- Business inventories
- Orders for new plant and equipment
- Building permits for new housing
- Incorporations of new businesses
- Companies experiencing delays in receiving orders from suppliers
- Average work week for manufacturing labor
- New orders for consumer goods
- New claims for unemployment insurance

Some of these statistics are measured in dollars, some in hours, and some as index numbers. The index of leading indicators assigns each component an equal weight, then arbitrarily sets 1982 equal to 100. Thus, if the index of leading indicators is 193 this month, it is 93 percent higher than it was in 1982.

Confused? You are not alone. The harder you stare at this index, the less it seems to mean. Probably the best way to use it is to look at the separate components. *If all of them, or almost all of them, are moving in the same direction, there is an excellent chance the economy will follow.* And the more months in a row they all move together and in the same direction, the more confidently one can assume they are right. On the other hand, if some are moving up and some are moving down, or if the index is bumping around from month to month, assume nobody knows what is happening.

International Finance

Merchandise Trade Balance. Reported monthly by the Commerce Department. Add up the dollars foreigners spend here for American goods. Then subtract the dollars Americans spend abroad on foreign goods. The difference is called the "merchandise trade balance."

If America exported $30 billion worth of corn and airplanes and chemicals last month and imported $25 billion worth of cars and cameras and oil, there would be a surplus in merchandise trade of $5 billion.

Such a surplus, by the way, would be quite unusual. Typically, the United States imports more goods than it exports, and is thus in deficit on merchandise trade. That's not necessarily bad: most countries go through long cycles of deficit and surplus that reflect both the costs of production and the purchasing power of investors and consumers. *What is bad, though, is a rapid change in the merchandise trade balance that reflects the collapse of specific industries.*

In the late 1970s the American steel, auto, and consumer electronics industries were all hit hard by import competition. In the early 1980s, the big losers included manufacturers of shoes and inexpensive clothing, and grain farmers. Workers lost their jobs. Suppliers lost business. Stock prices fell. Whole communities dependent on a few large employers were decimated.

It usually pays to avoid investments in companies that have lost their ability to compete in world markets. The profitability of such companies depends on the ability to get the government to protect them against imports. Once they get it, few ever manage to make it on their own again. And historically, few have even managed to prosper while on the government dole.

Current Account Balance. Reported quarterly by the Commerce Department. This one's a bit awkward to explain but worth the trouble to understand. *The current account is the international flow of money for purposes other than investment.* Merchandise trade, discussed above, is one big component. But it also includes (a) the sale and purchase of services, such as tourism, insurance, and banking; (b) interest paid and received on loans; (c) payments of dividends and profits to foreign stockholders; (d) government foreign aid; and (e) gifts to individuals—for example, the money immigrants send to relatives in the old country.

The current account offers a broad picture of how an

economy is managing its current finances with the rest of the world. If an economy's current account is in surplus—that is, if foreigners are sending more cash to pay for goods, services, interest, gifts, etc., than they are getting back—the economy is gradually accumulating IOUs from the rest of the world. On the other hand, if an economy's current account is in deficit, the country is living above its means and is gradually becoming indebted to the world. *Unless there is some mitigating circumstance, then, chronic current account deficits are bad news.* They can't go on forever. Eventually, a deficit country must reverse the flows, and typically, that means reducing its living standard.

Capital Account Balance. Reported quarterly by the Commerce Department. Add up all the money foreigners invest in America, everything from the purchase of U.S. Treasury bonds, to farmland in Iowa, to mutual fund shares. Subtract all the money Americans invest abroad. The resulting number is the "capital account balance."

Usually this number is broken down into short-term and long-term capital flows. Short-term capital is cash invested in bank accounts and other places where it can be withdrawn in a matter of hours or days without paying high commissions or penalties. Long-term capital is money locked into stocks or bonds, or the direct purchase of assets such as buildings or even whole companies.

The distinction is important because short-term capital moves restlessly from country to country in search of the highest interest rate or in speculation of a windfall gain associated with changes in exchange rates between currencies. *On the other hand, long-term capital movements usually reflect the work of more fundamental forces, such as the opportunity for profit from the operation of businesses.*

Notice that a surplus on our capital account would mean that foreigners invested more here than we did over there. Such a surplus is the mirror image of a deficit on the current account. When America's capital account is in deficit, people and companies abroad are accepting more dollars from Americans than they are sending back to pay for their purchases here. Those extra dollars, whether they sit around in the form of checking deposits at the Bank of America or are used to purchase IBM stock, represent investments in the United States.

If the foreigners were reluctant to hold these extra dollars in American investments, something would have to give. "Something," in this case, would be the exchange rate between dollars and foreign currencies. Americans who tried to buy things abroad would find they would have to pay more dollars to obtain the same terms. On the other hand, if foreigners were particularly eager to hold their savings in the form of dollars, Americans would find that foreign goods were cheap to buy.

PART THREE

The
Web

Surfing For Info

Reading the financial pages is a start. But active investors need more information to decide what to buy, how much and when—and many of them are turning to the Internet for help. The Internet—more specifically, the World Wide Web, which can be accessed through a home computer with a modem and an account with a commercial "Internet service provider"—is a cornucopia of information about investing. But the gold, alas, is rather thinly spread in the great sea of cyberspace, competing for attention with gossip, arcana, and useless trivia.

Here's a very selective list of great web sites for personal investors who range from rank amateur to been-there-done-that sophisticates. Only sites that are likely to last awhile on this rapidly changing medium have been included. And while some require surfers to pay for the privilege—this seems to be the wave of the future—many are supported solely by the little blocks of advertising that come with each screen of information, or payments for referrals to commercial web sites, or by spin-off products such as books.

Note that most of these sites contain links to other sites—which, after all, is why they call it the World Wide Web. Bounce around to your heart's content. But remember that nobody goes to the time, money, and trouble to maintain a web site without an ulterior motive. Putting it plainly, prudence pays: Start with the assumption that investment advice about specific mutual fund or securities recommendations is biased.

InvestorGuide (http://www.investorguide.com)

If I had to pick a single source of information about investing, this would probably be it. It offers tons of free material, plus hundreds of links to useful web sites. Among the gems are annotated lists of brokers, with all the info you need to pick the one suited to your needs.

Microsoft Investor (http://www.investor.msn.com)

Like everything else Microsoft does, this site is meant to be taken seriously. The site provides a flood of information, including constant news updates from the Microsoft Network and an ambitious personal finance "webzine." It's free, at least for now.

Stockmaster (http://www.stockmaster.com)

A lovely web site originally started at MIT that's chock-full of free information. It includes current price quotes, along with historical price data on thousands of stocks and mutual funds, plus trading data on top stocks and funds.

NETworth (http://www.networth.galt.com)

Another source of basic data on stocks and mutual funds. It includes free use of a "personal investment tracker" that lets you maintain comprehensive data on as many as 50 funds and stocks. NETworth also sells access to a variety of specialized databases including the Security and Exchange Commissioner's EDGAR service: a listing of documents that public companies are required to issue to create a level playing field for investors.

Investment Research (http://www.noc.thegroup.net/invest)

A little of this and a little of that, which add up to a lot. Basic data, articles about investing for both beginners and experts, plus capacity to create charts based on data you select are found here. And, at least for the moment, it's free.

Briefing by Chart Data (http://www.briefing.com)

Beautifully organized, easily accessible up-to-the-hour market data. The only catch is the monthly fee.

Disclosure (http://www.disclosure.com)

Investment pros use this service for one-stop shopping for disclosure documents from EDGAR and other sources. But anyone can use the neat financial calculator with step-by-step instructions on calculating everything from mortgage payments to bond yields.

The Syndicate (http://www.itnet.com/money pages/syndicate)

This is the pet project of Bill Rimi, a professional at both stock-picking and the design of web pages. The Syndicate is full of (constantly changing) goodies. Current strengths: mutual fund data and an endless list of specialized web sites for investors.

The Wall Street Journal Interactive (http://www.wsj.com).

This site is the *Wall Street Journal,* and then some. For a fee, you get a customized version of the daily newspaper (leaving out the stuff you don't want to read), plus vast amounts of investment reference materials, a 14-day archive of recent *Journal* articles, and a way of looking up just about anything from any other periodical.

Barron's (http://www.barrons.com)

The weekly tabloid bible of investment commentary and statistics has gone cyber. This is overkill for amateurs, but an extraordinary publication, nonetheless. Browse the site once to see if it's for you.

Fundmaster (http://www.fundmaster.com/yahoo.htm)

You can find lists of mutual funds, access to fund prospectuses, and a financial calculator on this site. Very easy to use and at no charge.

The Motley Fool (http://www.fool.com)

A great "webzine" for investors. The frequently updated site offers smart, very opinionated advice about the stock market, plus basics for novices. Begun as a lark, it has become an industry, with lots of investment books and other commercial ventures to its credit. Read, enjoy—but don't take it as gospel.

American Association of Individual Investors (http://www.aaii.org)

The home page of a fine, nonprofit organization dedicated to providing high-quality impartial information to the nonprofessional. Not glitzy, but rock solid. Check out this free site.

EduStock (http://tqd.advanced.org/3088)

Like many good web sites, its strength is in its flexibility. EduStock stands out for its company profiles and its stimulation game. The game gives you $100,000 in play money, then tests your skills at trading securities using real data from the markets.

Stock Smart (http://www.stocksmart.com)

This page is loaded with data, including current quotes on foreign as well as domestic securities. The neat feature here is a mutual fund "search wizard," that ranks some 5,000 funds and lets you sort through them by various criteria.

All clear? Don't worry if it's still a little blurry around the edges. Even the pros take months to learn the jargon by heart. Just keep *How to Read the Financial Pages* nearby for easy reference.

About the Author

PETER PASSELL is the author of the highly acclaimed books *Where to Put Your Money* and *Personalized Money Strategies*. Currently a financial columnist for the *New York Times,* he has been published in numerous magazines and has explained the intricacies of finance on many radio and television shows including *Latenight America, Larry King,* and *Independent Network News.* Holder of a Ph.D. in economics from Yale University, he is a former Professor at Columbia University.